Messages From Nature's Guardians

Fairy Wishes

Tracy
x

Cover image graciously supplied by
Josephine Wall

ISBN 0-9528531-2-4

Messages From Nature's Guardians

Fiona Murray

www.elementalbeings.co.uk

Dedication

To the wonderful beings of the Elemental realm,
with thanks for everything you do for the planet.

Contents

Foreword
Introduction

After Word
Elemental Tour Of Scotland
Acknowledgements

Foreword

Messages From Nature's Guardians sees popular speaker turned author, Fiona Murray unveil her unusual ability to communicate with the Elemental realms. Journey with her to other dimensions, normally unseen by us mere mortals! Strong messages about the results of our actions towards the environment come through very convincingly. You will experience Fiona's passion for these realms and gain insights into the way she manages to communicate with these beings that dwell beyond the gossamer veil in another magical yet very real dimension. This book is a real inspiration and helps us to see that each and every one of us can connect with these beautiful unseen realms, if we so desire. The Faeries and other Elementals really do want to help us to understand their plight as guardians of the land. In a way we are all joint tenants on this planet and we need to live and work in harmony to really ensure a bright future for our beautiful home. I wholeheartedly recommend this beautiful and insightful book.

Editor in Chief , Fae Magazine

This is a mystical and magical book, weaving timelessly throughout the fairy glens of Scotland and connecting us back to the guardians of this ancient land. By every stone, tree, loch and mountain lives a wisdom-keeper patiently awaiting our return helping us to unlock that which has been forgotten but not lost, so that we all can access the worlds of spirit both seen and unseen. When you read *Messages From Nature's Guardians* the Elementals dance right out of the pages, so best you read this book in Nature so that you can experience the world of the Faey. Fiona is a wonderful storyteller and seer, holds great honour and respect for our ancestors. A blessing indeed.

Barbara Miekeljohn-Free
The Highland Seer and author of *The Heart Of All Knowing*

Introduction

*"I have come to tell you, you will write a book," a booming voice
said to me. I knew who it was. He had visited me before. A book on what I
thought? It was then my spiritual journey truly began...*

It is important to point out that until recently I had no knowledge
of Elementals; also known as Nature Spirits. I did not know
what they were, what they did or where to find them. Spirituality
was not something I was interested in during the early time of my
life. As a child I was very driven, interested in learning and
participating in sport. I do remember however that from an early
age I was always fascinated by nature; why a mountain was shaped
a certain way, why a river had chosen that particular path to the
sea and the sheer unpredictability and power of earthquakes,
volcanoes and tornadoes.

At University I studied Physical Geography with Environmental
Studies and took Politics as my outside course. Career wise, my
aim was to make Scotland's precious and beautiful environment
better protected. I thought at the time the way to do this was by
becoming an environmental lobbyist, which I did after
graduating.

However after contracting a serious life-threatening illness,
similar to meningitis, at the age of 23, which left me bed ridden
and unable to move for over a year, I found my clairaudience
opened up; a sixth sense I never knew I had before which gave me
the ability to hear beings in other realms! I was then told by the
Angels, who I was now able to hear and speak to, that it was
through writing books that I could make the difference.

Yes, the booming voice I heard that day was the voice of
Archangel Metatron. I followed his advice and started to write
down the spiritual experiences I had over the next few weeks.
After doing this I could then clearly see the book he had in

mind for me; to use my newly found spiritual gifts and my environmental knowledge to give voice to the beings of the Elemental realm: Nature's Guardians. During this time of change on planet Earth it would be allowing them to tell their story, as well as me telling mine.

Further Reading

If at any point during your journey through this book or after reading it you would like to know more about the following:

❖ Fairies and Elementals workshops and talks
❖ Animal Communication
❖ Guardian Angel Workshops and talks
❖ Manifesting Abundance with Angels and Fairies Workshops
❖ Unicorn Workshops
❖ Archangel Workshops
❖ Tools to help you connect with Elementals, Angels, Goddesses and Ascended Masters.
❖ Channelled meditations.

Then please do feel free to visit

❖ www.elementalbeings.co.uk to see the events diary or request a workshop in your area.
❖ www.alphedia.co.uk/shop
❖ Channelled messages at www.alphedia.co.uk/blog
❖ For information on Romany visit www.thothdog.co.uk

© Richard Kenchington

© Myrea Pettit

Chapter 1
First Elementals - The Fairies

I begin this book by introducing the Elemental group with whom my whole experience of working and communicating with the nature spirits began - the Fairies. Everybody knows about Fairies from stories such as Peter Pan, yet not everybody believes they exist. As a child I held a secret hope that they did. It wasn't until I was 26 however, that I found out they really did; just not in 'our' physical realm. In this book many secrets and powers that the Elementals possess will be made clear.

This chapter explains the Fairies' role on Earth and how to bring Fairies into your life along with the benefits of doing so. Each subsequent chapter will introduce a different Elemental group; their roles and the help they need from humans to better protect the environment. They also teach us how we can work with them to heal ourselves.

Writing this book I feel very privileged to have met so many wonderful beings and wish to thank them now for their assistance, cooperation and especially for the many healings which have aided my recovery enormously.

The Elementals play a vital role in safeguarding our continued existence as a race on Earth and I hope, by writing this book, to raise awareness of the Elemental Kingdom, to highlight how our lifestyles are impacting on the natural environment and to encourage people to feel as passionately about protecting it as I do. Most of all, the Elementals' messages have made me see that all is not lost for this planet. There are things we can do to turn round the current state of imbalance and pollution that Mother Earth is suffering from. If we work with the Elementals we, as well as the environment, will benefit from healing within all areas of our lives.

What Are Fairies?

Fairies have long been in Scottish folklore and children's tales and I wasn't fully aware of what Fairies were when I had my first conscious Elemental experience. I am sure as a child I probably met Fairies but the remembrance of any encounter has long disappeared from my memory. As children, many people often see and experience relationships with Fairies until the reality of their existence is knocked out of them, mostly by disbelieving adults. However, Fairies are real, just not in our physical dimension. When working with Fairies and Elementals we are using our sixth sense. A sense we all have but don't develop in the same way we do our other five senses. As young children our sixth sense is usually more open because we have not yet been conditioned by society in what is acceptable and what is not.

Although Fairies are associated with children I have learnt that they have a very important environmental role to play on earth. This is because Fairies are the Plant Guardians. They tend to blades of grass, rose bushes and flowering plants to name a few. Each plant has a different kind of Fairy as its guardian; a bit like you and I have our own Guardian Angels who keep us from harm and guide us in the right direction to fulfil our life's path. All you need to work with Fairies is a true belief in their existence.

The Fairies I have met appear as would expect; beautiful little beings with wings and brightly coloured costumes. Of course at the start I could not see them. It is only now after a year and a half of working with them that I can see them in all their glory. There are two types of Fairies that I have met; Plant Fairies and Flower Fairies. Flower Fairies live on the flowering plants and usually wear the colour of their plant's flower for their attire. They have squeaky voices and very excitable, joyful energy which is uplifting to be around. If you are out in nature and find yourself bursting out in laugher or getting the giggles then you have probably stumbled upon Fairy energy as they often demonstrate their presence to us in that way.

My First Meeting

I have to admit the first time I went to try and find Fairies I felt a bit stupid. I had not long been able to walk outside and had always needed a companion. This day I decided to go outside myself. There was a grass park a short distance from my parent's house so I walked there and went to a bush with flowers on it. I had read a book on Fairies by an Angel author who I enjoyed reading very much and I decided to go and see if, like her, I could talk to them. I already knew my spiritual gift was clairaudience because I could hear and speak to Archangels and my Guardian Angels. I firmly believed in the existence of Angels so why not Fairies!

I tried clearing my mind and I concentrated my intent on communicating with the flower guardians of the bush. I then consciously sent out love to them from my heart. I heard and saw nothing. Disappointment quickly filtered through me. I had found speaking with Angels relatively easy with my first attempt. Disappointment was swiftly joined by self-consciousness (people might see me and wonder what I was doing). All the neighbours knew how ill I had been and most probably thought they would not see me walking again, so were likely to come over for a chat. I decided to try again somewhere else. However as I was leaving I became aware I was being watched by unseen eyes. I knew they were there. My disappointment lifted and a strong belief in their existence kicked in as I walked away. This belief grew over the following days as did my faith that I had the ability to speak to them. It would just be matter of time until it happened. As it turned out it was the next time I tried!

Fairies In The Carrot Field

My first successful Fairy encounter was in a carrot field. At that time I had started to work a few hours as an environmental consultant and part of my remit was to help with the agricultural section of the business. I decided to the fields to see if I could communicate or meet with the Fairies on the carrot crop. My visit was on a sunny summer's afternoon and when I entered the field and tried to tune into their realm I was still unable to see or hear them however I could sense their presence like the first time. I now know that Fairies can be a bit timid at first, and will only communicate with you once they sense you are not going to cause them harm. This quite is understandable in a carrot field I suppose when you don't know if the person walking into the field is there to give you and your home a nasty dose of chemicals! After a minute of standing amongst the carrots I started laughing. Richard, who is now my partner, was with me and started to smile too. He was also unable to hear them but felt uplifted by their joyfulness. I tuned in deeper into the Fairy realm by focusing my intent and losing the awareness of my physical surroundings. I then started to hear laughter and became aware of beings flitting about around me. I left the carrot field that day with the sense that the Fairies were happy with the work we were doing for them and their environment. I also felt an excitement again in my life which had been missing for three years.

As I have alluded to my ability to clearly hear Angels had developed greatly the more I recovered from the viral infection (the cause of my M.E.) that had so nearly taken my life. I had been bedridden and unable to move for six months when I had a near death experience. The doctors did not know what was wrong with me as they had never carried out a meningitis test and all other neurological tests had come back negative at this point. I remember my near death experience vividly. I had started going into a coma. I was lying on a hospital bed, in my bedroom, trying to shout for help but couldn't get words out. I kept thinking I must summon up the energy from deep inside to open my eyes, but they would not open. I could still hear my mother and father around me but I could not respond. The next thing I knew I was above my bed looking down on my body and my parents when I heard a deep voice say, "*You have a choice: to live or to die.*" There was no hesitation when I made the choice. I said in my head,

"*I don't want to die yet.*" I was then back in my body and my mother slapped the left side of my face. With that, I was awake.

I remember it all as if it had been yesterday. I have since been told by Archangel Metatron that by making the choice to live and continue on my divine mission, God had granted me more psychic powers to help with my work. He said I had been given the choice whether to die because they could not allow me to suffer in the amount of pain I was in unless I was willing. I believe that partly my illness was an opportunity for me to awaken spiritually and get on my path. I have read this has happened to others also. I truly believe that an Angel spoke to me that moment when I was out of my body and since that day they have worked to bring two healing Earth Angels into my life to aid my recovery. It was not long after that experience that my communications with my Guardian Angels and the Archangels have become everyday experiences and life has become much easier through working with them. I have also found a lot of joy in working with the Elemental realm.

After about my third trip to the carrot field I started to be able to see the Fairies in my clairvoyant eye. There were thousands of them all busily working away at the carrot tops. And it was during that third visit, that I heard the first Elemental speak to me. I asked no Fairy in particular if the carrots were growing well and if they were happy. I then heard a squeaky voice of one of the Fairies say, "*Yes, yes we are happy thank you, the carrots are doing well.*" Since then every time when I returned to the carrot field I would crouch and have a chat with them about what they needed to help the carrots grow well. They would say when they needed water or more silica even one time they asked for more sun! Towards the end of the growing season I decided to ask what happens to them when the fields are sprayed and the carrots are lifted. A Fairy, larger than any I'd met before, appeared and said, "*If we have two days notice of spraying or lifting, we can all get out of the way.*" Elementals like humans like to have warnings of changes about to occur in their lives especially if we humans are going to be damaging or change their homes. Try to get into the habit of talking to the Fairies before you are about to cut your grass, cut your garden flowers or even pick some apples. You do not need to say it out loud. It is just courteous to let them know what you are about to do to their plant and possibly their homes. The Fairies will thank you and reward you for your courteousness by helping your plants grow better and prettier.

Their Role On Earth

The Fairies have explained to me that their Divine mission on this planet is to protect the natural environment and particularly the plants. They called out to me as an environmentalist because we share the same love for nature. Fairies as a race bestow many gifts to humans they have explained to me, for example they tend to a flower from bud to produce a beautiful display of colour and scent for us, yet few humans take the time to these days appreciate the experience. We regularly destroy their homes when we spray weed killer, pesticides and fertilisers on them and interfere with the natural process of plant growth. The Fairies explained to me they are particularly sensitive to man made chemicals many of which are sprayed over plants and crops frequently. The plants are the Fairies' homes so anything that is done to a plant affects its Fairy guardians too. They have described it to me that it is a bit like someone going and spraying paint all over the front of your house that you have been keeping tidy and well cared for.

All Fairies are gifted with the power to heal not only plants that are struggling but humans and animals also. Of all the Elementals, the Fairies have the greatest affinity for human beings. They are particularly good at healing wounded human hearts by using their gift of replacing sadness with joy and do this by pouring Divine Love into the hearts of those who ask and are open to receiving their Fairy gifts. They are delighted when we talk with them; having so much wisdom to pass on to us regarding our co-guardianship of Earth. By spending time

18

outdoors with the Fairies we can learn a lot as they show us how to truly love all creatures equally.

Fairies live in a dimension which is close to the physical one we live in. This means Fairies and Elementals are vulnerable to the effects of lifestyle choices of human beings because they rely on us for the co-guardianship of their homes - the plants. Therefore they are particularly concerned by human interference in the plant kingdom such as the advent of genetically modified crops. They urge us to campaign and protest against man-made crops because they can and will have a disastrous effect on our natural vegetation. Also if we humans did not spray our crops with such damaging chemicals and instead called on the Fairies for help with any growth problems and lived more in harmony with nature we would have no use for such products.

Some of you are probably already environmentally conscious however the Fairies desperately want us to pay more attention to the produce we buy. Each individual who makes a stance against G.M.O. crops and buys organic fruit and vegetables is making a difference to the planet and the Fairies. The Fairies also explained that they play an important role in the soil eco-system and programme certain plants to grow in specific areas to try to maintain the natural balance. Often weeds that grow in a crop field are naturally counteracting the imbalances or deficiencies in a certain patch of soil. So we are causing further problems by spraying pesticides onto these plants we term as weeds. The Fairies are urgently calling at this time for a return to more natural farming methods in particular.

In my conversations with different Fairies in various locations they have all urged me spread their message of protecting their homes and our planet. Fairies love to work with humans who care as much for the environment as they do. Of course Fairies have many healing roles for human beings. Later chapters will discuss how working with the Fairies can improve your health, manifest your desires and heal the heart of trauma. I have experienced so much enjoyment since I started to acknowledge

Fairies in my life. Working with the Elemental realm can bring light and happiness into your life too. Let me take you on this special journey of discovery into the realm of the Elementals - Nature's Guardians

Appreciation & Invocation

I would like to thank Maeve, one of the Fairy Queens for her assistance with this chapter. Maeve is not a Fairy on earth. She is among a group that are called Goddesses. They live in a realm in the ethers similar to Angels. Maeve is my main guide in writing this book. She has always been available to answer my questions about the Fairy world and she has guided me to various locations to meet different Nature Guardians. To communicate with Maeve yourself call her when outdoors or amongst flowers by saying:

"Beloved Maeve, Queen of the Fairies, may I please ask for your help with (insert your problem). Please help me to enhance and increase my communications with the Fairies. My wish is to help protect my environment and for my garden/park/woodland to flourish. Assign me a task to help aid the Fairies' mission of creating a harmoniously balanced environment for all. Thank you Maeve for your help".

© Judy Mastrangelo

21

© Myrea Pettit

Chapter 2
Animal Guardians - The Pixies

Having met the Fairies in the carrot field I knew I could communicate with the Nature Guardians. This was why I had studied the environment at University and I knew I had to write a book about them. I was unsure really what this would involve, how long it would take to do and most importantly of all, who the other Elementals were. I had no idea where to find them or what to say to them. There was also an element of fear within me. Being a 'Scot' I had heard the folklore tales of mischievous nature spirits, yet at the same time this did not feel right to me. I had felt nothing but warmth and love from the Fairies and I had a strong feeling that in these folklore tales the Elementals had been misrepresented. I was still undergoing treatment to aid my recovery, learning to walk further and it was therefore a couple of months after I had spoken to the Fairies that I met my second type of Elemental, the Pixies who guard animals. They live in the same dimension as the Fairies, they even look like Fairies, but have smaller wings, and the first one I met is the guardian of Romany, my partner Richard's little black dog.

Communication

You can communicate with animals by speaking to their Pixie guardian. If a pet is lost you can call to their guardian to send them home or send your Guardian Angel to their Pixie with a message to guide them to you. I have used this method often with Romany. When Romany turned one year old he started to wander. As Richard lived near the top of a hill surrounded by forests and heather it is hard to find a little black 'snoodle' dog. I therefore sent my Guardian Angel to where he was. You can do this by simply saying to your Guardian Angel *"I have a message for you to deliver to the guardian of (pet's name)"*. I am clairaudient so was able to hear my Angel saying to me that he was at the bottom of the hill, near the river. So we got into the land rover and drove down the hill but could not see him anywhere.

I asked his Pixie guardian and the Angels to keep him safe, truly believing they would. I then turned to Richard and said I think we should go back to the house. When we got in the front door the telephone was ringing. A lady had found him in the main road of the village as she was driving to work and thought she should stop and pick him up. We drove down to meet her and saw her standing with Romany in her arms. As she handed him over she said, *"Don't give him a row please, he is a gorgeous dog."* I then saw bright sparks flashing around her. I know that Angels show themselves to people in this way. I took this as a sign that she was an Earth Angel called to rescue our dog and an answer to my prayers to keep him safe.

Romany had managed to cross the bridge over the River Tweed and had wandered along the farm track to the main road. It is my belief that the Angels had heard my request to keep him safe and had worked with Romany's Pixie to guide Romany to this lady. Angels often guide people to go to certain locations or to do certain things and can drop ideas into our heads such as *"I had better stop and see if that dog is ok."* The Pixies' role is to do the same for the animal they are assigned to protect. Romany's Pixie told me at times he has difficulty controlling him as he often ignores his guardian's advice. That made me laugh, dogs and humans are no different then in not always heeding the advice of their guides!

I believe it is also possible to communicate with wild and farmed animals through their Pixie guides. Once we were driving along a rural road and came upon cows that were being herded along the road to another field. When the cows met the Land Rover they did not know where to go and were starting to panic. There was plenty of room to the right of us but they were all heading to the left or straight towards the car. I said to my Angel, *"Please speak to the cows' guardians and guide them safely to the right of the vehicle. There is plenty of room there."* In an instant the cows turned and started moving right safely around the car. There was then an air of peace because the cows were no longer panicking and neither was I that they might trample the new vehicle!

Healing Role Of Animals

Pixies are like Fairies in having healing powers for humans as well as for their animals. This is why when we play with animals and stroke or pet them we often get a sense of peace or a sense of pain relief. Interacting with an animal means you are interacting with its Pixie too. I have also discovered that just as there are Earth Angels incarnate as humans there are Earth Elementals too.

We knew Romany was a healing dog. In the same way my pet rabbit as a child was a healing rabbit. Muffat was white with black ears, feet and tail. He had special hyper-allergenic fur similar to Romany and from an early age he received lots of love and attention. Due to this he would follow us at heel about the house and garden. He would respond to being called and would wait at the back door to be let out when he needed the toilet. As a child I was often ill, being asthmatic and more susceptible to colds and flu. In the winter, Muffat would hop into the kitchen to get his breakfast. One morning I was off school ill and my bedroom door was open. Muffat ran from the kitchen into the bedroom and jumped up onto my bed. This was quite a feat for a little rabbit. He then came and lay on my chest. I did not realise at the time but I know now that he and his Pixie were healing me. Often when I was seriously ill I would lie in my bed and wish that Muffat was still alive to come and lie with me because he would quite happily do so for hours whilst being cuddled.

Many animals are sent to earth with a special healing role for the certain person they become attached to. These animals tend to want to be stroked lots and radiate love and joy in fulfilling their life's mission as a pet. I believe that they are sent to heal, provide companionship and sometimes, to show that particular soul what unconditional love is. Pets also provide lots of joy and a reminder to us of the importance of playfulness. I believe that anyone can speak to animals and their guardians however they will only respond if you do it from a place of love. Also remember when you are communicating with Elementals that they are highly sentient and can feel what you are feeling towards them and they will know if you are not doing things from a place of love.

Animal Telepathy

Many of you are likely to have a pet, perhaps a dog, cat or rabbit. It is best to try speaking to their Pixie for the first time when they are calm, perhaps whilst being petted. In order to see your pet's Pixie try to relax yourself and consciously will yourself to see with your third eye which is situated in the middle of your forehead. Do not worry if you see nothing. Practice makes perfect. You will all have different skills and specialties when it comes to your sixth sense. Mine is my ability to hear etheric beings, some of you may be able to sense them and know how they are feeling, called clairsentience, others among you may just 'know' (claircognisance). This knowing will come as if from nowhere but this is actually an Angel or Elemental dropping a thought into your mind. I think it is easier first to start to communicate with one particular Elemental or group of Elementals. You will learn about the different groups of Elementals in this book and in which habitat to find them. You can then choose the Elementals that you personally wish to have a relationship with or which ones you would like to work with in healing the planet. Most likely they will pick you.

It is easiest however with animal communication, to start with ones that you are around regularly. Often as pet owners we wish to speak to our pets and know what they are thinking. My experience is that if you have advanced clairaudience you can do just that. I also believe it is possible for every one of us to develop our clairaudience with practice and time. Just like we can learn to read and we learn to write. You are just one step away from talking directly to animals when you speak to its Pixie. Animals, you see, like humans have what are called higher and lower selves. Our higher self is the part that is always in tune with the spiritual realm, the part that travels elsewhere on the spiritual plane when we sleep and can always remember what we have learnt in the other realms. It is the part of us that communicates with Angels and Elementals. The challenge for souls incarnate on earth is to integrate the higher and lower self. If we just work with our lower selves we have no connection with Angels, Elementals and other spiritual beings while we are on the physical plane. We are driven by emotions, reactions and our egos. We lose sight of the over picture and the reason why we each individually incarnated and have connection to the Divine (the source of all that is). When the lower and higher self are integrated it is possible for us to work with the other realms and live according to our divine path.

I appreciate that this might be confusing and difficult initially to get one's head around if you have not read any of what is called spiritual literature. I know because I had not! But one day I could tell that I was not talking to Romany's Pixie but to Romany's higher self because the voice I could hear was not squeaky and it bizarrely sounded like I would expect him to sound like if he could physically talk. In the past this communication form was called telepathy. Telepathy is when two people's higher selves communicate through thought alone. The day I realised Romany was telepathically talking to me was when one night I asked him if he was alright. Just the same as most of you probably ask your pets when you think they are unwell or not themselves.

Romany is usually very boisterous and playful but all night he had been lethargic and sleepy. So I asked him what was wrong, was he just tired? To my surprise and delight he replied grumpily saying, "No, *I have bellyache because I ate some sheep poo and feel very unwell.*" I asked what I could do to help him and he replied saying he wanted some warm milk. Richard said he doesn't drink much and he has never had milk. We gave him a big bowl of milk and he lapped it all down. Then he looked at me and said, *"A bit more please!"* After he had drunk a second bowl and lain down for a bit I sensed he was feeling better but wanted out. I asked if he wanted to go out and he said, *"Yes I am desperate."* I realised then I was really talking to a dog! We now communicate this way regularly. I know it is him not his Pixie because the voice is different and he speaks from his own personal point of view.

Pixies Under The Water

I had been told that Pixies also guard fish. I had no way of finding out if this was true until one day Richard came home from work with a bag of freshwater mussels which he had been given by a shellfish farmer. Technically a mussel is not a fish but I thought I would try and see if its guardian would speak to me. Mussels are still alive when they are sold so I took one of the mussels and placed it in a bowl of water to which I added sea salt so the mussel would feel more at home. Part of the Pixie's job is to provide love and reassurance to its charge just as this is a Guardian Angel's job for a human. To my delight when I addressed the guardian of the mussel the Pixie protecting this mussel said to me, *"I am the Pixie guardian of this mussel. We Pixies don't have wings. My job is to guard this animal and the soul within during its incarnation as a mussel. All sea dwelling creatures have a guardian. Fish have Pixies too. The mussel is an important sea dweller because it filters the water. It means that if the water is polluted with a chemical or bacteria the mussel will swallow it. That is why people can become very unwell when eating seafood that is not fresh and cooked properly. It is very important at this time to get the state of the sea sorted. It is in real trouble due to global warming, pollution and tidal changes,"* the Pixie explained to me. This message made me think about how we as the human race are impacting on the Elementals through their protection roles of animals. Maeve had told me about how human activities are impacting on Fairy life and now

28

the mussel Pixie was telling me how humans impact on Pixies through indirect action too.

The Pixie had intrigued me by saying it guarded the soul in the mussel through its life being a mussel, implying that unlike an Angel it did not stay with it after death. So I asked about that part of the message. The Pixie told me, *"We are usually just with an animal through one incarnation because not all souls choose to be that animal again."* This Pixie was posing new ideas that I was finding hard to comprehend. It was like Maeve had said, by writing this book part of me, either my memory or my consciousness, (which I wasn't sure at this point) was being awakened. I asked what he looked like. *"We are fatter than Fairies, and usually are male in appearance to humans but not always. Water-dwelling Pixies do not usually have wings. Pixies like to have fun which is why animals have a playful nature at large. Obviously a mussel does not, it lives in a shell!"* This made me smile. The Elementals I had met so far certainly were more exuberant than any Angel I had met! Speaking to the mussel Pixie had aroused my curiosity about what other Elementals lived in the water environment. My excitement was increasing about unfolding this secret world of nature spirits that had only been alluded to as reality in the tales of Scotland's folklore. I was excited now at where this journey would lead me.

Appreciation & Invocation

Thank you to Brigit, Irish Goddess who is a protector of animals, for her help in writing this chapter. To invoke Brigit to help you to communicate with animals, she has asked you to say:

"Beloved Brigit, I ask for your help communicating with animals and Pixies. I share your love of all God's creatures and I wish to commune and help animals. I ask you to assign me divine missions in which I can work with and protect these remarkable beings for the good of all. Thank you Brigit."

© Hayley Rust

Chapter 3
Dancing With Sprites

With my curiosity aroused by the mussel Pixie about Elementals living in water I decided that to meet my third Elemental group I would go to the river. I did not have to go far as Richard lived near the River Tweed, however I had little idea or clue about which Elemental I might find there. The way forward was to ask a Goddess who had a particular interest in water or Elementals to help me. As well as being able to communicate with Angels and Elementals, I could now communicate with Goddesses too; Maeve as you know had helped me with the Fairies and Brigit had helped with the Pixies. I decided to contact Diana, a moon Goddess who has a special connection with Elementals. I asked her to guide and assist me in contacting the water Elementals. Diana is a high priestess, which means she is one of the ancient Goddesses. She was worshiped in Roman times and you can still find temples today that have shrines in her honour.

What Diana told me was that Sprites, which appear much like little men with webbed feet and short hair (often sporting beards), are the Elementals that look after the freshwater environment. They are very playful and you will often hear or feel their excitable energy especially near shallow fast flowing water such as a stream. You also will find Sprites in the surf and near waterfalls. If you ever notice sparks in the water but know it's not fish causing them, then you will be witnessing Sprites playing. They are both joyous and mischievous Elementals. They do not have the same healing role for humans as Pixies or Fairies but just being in their presence can uplift your spirits. Water Sprites look after rivers and are guardians of many animals that live within. Diana told me that Sprites would be easier to find in fast flowing water. That's good, I thought, as there is a fast flowing stream by the side of the house, there must be Sprites living there!

Environmental Concerns

I was really looking forward to meeting the Sprites. I have always held an affinity with water. It is my favourite element. When I was a child my grandparents lived on a small farm which had a water mill and a 'burn' (Scottish term for a small water feature such as a creek or stream) flowing around it and a lade to turn the water wheel. As a child I would spend hours playing in the burn. I remember it always had a very special feeling and it always seemed to me to be a very magical place. I have sometimes felt that magic around other streams but not all of them. Although there are Sprites in every wetland there are more in natural settings where there has been less interference through building and pollution. I have since found out that like Fairies, the magical powers of Sprites are affected by chemicals and other pollutants that end up in our waterways. It made sense that more Sprites would choose to live in a clean healthy wetland surrounded by other Elementals. If you or I had the choice to live next to a beautiful river with lots of trees and plants around or one that was brown with pollution, full of litter or shop trolleys which would you choose?

Diana informed me that the Sprites are an Elemental group very susceptible to human mismanagement of their homes. Water pollution affects Sprites greatly. Scotland is a country which has, what many would consider to be, pristine waterways. However agriculture is a large land use and causes pollution due to the current conventional farming methods. Diana said the Sprites main environmental concerns are chemicals in the water and acid rain. Runoff from chemicals placed in the fields disrupts the harmony of wetlands and causes algal growths, sometimes poisonous, to occur across the top of the 'loch' (Scottish term for lake) or river. This suffocates any life below the water through starvation of oxygen. Acid rain affects the pH of wetlands meaning that the local ecosystems are completely out of balance, fish die off, plants shrivel up and decay, and the waterways become barren and devoid of life as happened in Scandinavia in the 1990s. Humans often interfere by adding more chemicals and substances such as lime, to try to neutralise the effects of the pollution. However, the Sprites have told me during our conversations that this can often compound the situation, creating a greater problem.

It is important therefore we humans take care to protect our precious wetlands. The Sprites urge us to use environmentally friendly washing up liquid and soap detergents. They are also concerned by what we place down the toilet. All personal and sanitary products should always be placed in the bin. Often major manufacturing companies discharge waste straight into rivers. It is important that we lobby to stop this process. Organisations such as Friends of the Earth and the Royal Society for the Protection of Birds (RSPB) work to try to pressure governments into curtailing these activities and to return the Earth back to natural balance. In many countries raw sewage is still discharged straight into the sea with disastrous consequences to wildlife. Clean rivers, streams and lochs are very important for the health of the Earth and human beings. Have you felt revitalised after a walk along a clean riverbank or just sitting quietly by a loch? When the environment is in harmony our human bodies are too.

Romany's Sprite Encounter

I had been working with the Sprites for over a week now; being in their presence, feeling their energy and listening to them. We took Romany to the river with us for a walk. Animals can have the ability to see into other realms also and Romany definitely has the gift which can cause great amusement on walks with him. I decided to try and find some Sprites. I sensed their presence in a fast flowing part of the stream. Romany was off running about in the long grass in the opposite direction. I saw Water Sprites jumping about in the stream and as I stood and watched them joyfully playing they said, *"We love it when the water is high and the stream is fast. We can jump and slide down the rapids"*. Like the

Fairies they have squeaky voices and it sounded like two or three were speaking at the same time. Then Romany appeared running at the rate of knots about to jump into the stream, when all of a sudden he stopped at the water's edge. He stood stalk still and was staring at the spot where the cluster of Sprites were. They stopped playing and were staring back at him. Romany moved a paw and I heard them say, *"Do not cross here dog"*. He stood staring for a moment and then walked off subdued in the other direction. He often stops suddenly when we walk him in the forest and just stares. Now I think it must be some Elementals telling him to go no further!

Sprites And Ley Lines

In my experience more Sprites are found in streams which run along a ley line or an energy zone. Ley lines are energy lines where the energy deep within the earth rises up to the surface. You find that when you stand on a ley line, you can feel the Earth energy rush into your body. More Elementals accumulate around these high energy zones and so strengthen the available healing energy of the Earth at these points. One of the most magical places I have ever visited was Gulfoss waterfall in Iceland. It is the largest waterfall in Europe, formed by a giant jolkhaulp: a massive glacial flood caused by a volcano erupting under an icecap. I realise now that the feeling I got when I stood at the edge of this thundering waterfall with the spray soaking my face and hair, was that of being in the presence of millions of Water Sprites dancing and playing in the rushing water. Iceland is one of the few countries in the world where you can be so closely in touch with Mother Earth's energy. This country formed from underwater volcanoes erupting where two plates separate at the Mid-Atlantic ridge. The geology is continually evolving and changing. After my visit to the waterfall my energy levels soared and I felt replenished for the first time in weeks. I was, at that point, only just recovering from glandular fever and the tiredness associated with it. The Elementals have explained to me that it is very beneficial for human beings, when recovering from illness especially, to spend time in nature. They will heal you whether you ask or not, just being in their environment is enough.

Energetic Cleaners

About five months after meeting my first Sprites we were again walking Romany along the banks of the River Tweed. The river was relatively low and I was walking along part of the river bed when I heard the Sprites calling me. I stopped and stared at the water. *"I can't see any of you just now,"* I said back. *"Look into the surf. Can you feel the surf feels more magical than the lagoon bits?"* they asked me. I nodded in agreement. There was a distinct energetic difference. *"Well that's because not that many of us reside in the slow water. We gather our healing energy from the energetic force generated by the quick movement over the stones that create the rapids,"* the Sprites explained. I asked the Sprites what it was they do for the water. The answer given to me was very interesting.

The Sprite replied, *"What we do for the water is to energetically purify it. Healing waters are water in wells that have special Sprites called Delphinions; who's job it is to put the healing frequencies into the waters. There are thousands of Delphinions at Lourdes in France which is why it is renowned for healing. The energetic healing frequencies that the Elementals harness and put into the earth heal the plants, animals and humans too."* The Sprite continued, *"In clean rivers, lots of Sprites purify the water frequencies energetically. In polluted areas the Sprites powers of healing are hampered by the debris and pollution in the water. It is too dense for us to cope with. The rivers were never meant to get so dirty. When rivers are dirty the energy of the land and everything around is lowered. This energy depletion means that disease and illness sets in."* I pondered on this statement. Though my degree was in physical geography, I studied human geography in my first year, looking at how people living next to landfill sites, power stations and in areas of heavy pollution suffered more ill health, thereby proving a link between environmental factors and social factors such as health. Complementary practitioners, like homeopaths and herbalists, seek the cause of the disease rather than just treating the symptoms as with most conventional practices. There is also the theory that it is 'energetic blockages' causing disease which manifest into physical form within the body.

What the Sprite was saying was incredibly interesting because we as humans can feel the difference in the energy walking along a dirty river or a clean one. I could easily comprehend a dirty, polluted dense waterway, meandering through a beautiful valley impacting all the trees, plants and flowers around it, as well as the humans and animals nearby. The Sprite finished by saying, *"Rivers are meant to be energy purifiers so we Sprites play a vital role in the energy systems of all the ecosystems in the world."* I thanked the Sprites of the River Tweed for giving me greater understanding of their roles and a deeper understanding water pollution. I now had knowledge of the plant, animal and freshwater guardians and what they did on Earth, as well as the ways they enhanced life for the human race, albeit mostly unknown and unacknowledged by us. Which Elemental group would present itself to me next?

Appreciation & Invocation

Thank you Goddess Diana also known as Artemis, high priestess, for helping me with this chapter. To invoke Diana for assistance say:

"Diana, Princess on high, please come to me now as I sit by this riverbed (or whatever waterway you are by). Please help me to see, hear and feel your beautiful Sprites. Please open my heart so I may feel their love and please help me to communicate more with all Elementals. I care for and wish to protect the planet. Please give me any task I can do to further your cause. Thank you for your communications Diana."

© Wendy Andrew

37

© Hayley Rust

Chapter 4
Beings In The Fire

The next Elemental to enter my consciousness took me by surprise. I had read a book which briefly mentioned Elementals called Salamanders. I had paid no real attention to it however as there was not much written about them. Then, one night, as I was sitting by the open fire I became aware of presences in the flames.

This is often the first way I know an Elemental is about. I sense them. It was a very, very windy night in November and the flames were licking up. I was at the time alone in the living room. Since no one was about to ask what I was doing I said aloud, "*Who are you?*" I then heard a voice talk back! It was not squeaky like the Fairies and Sprites had been. It was a more masculine tone. The answer I received was, "*You have just become aware of Salamanders!*"

I racked my brains then remembered they had been mentioned in a book I had read. At this point in my Elemental journey I still was a bit sceptical to the existence of some of these beings. I had accepted Fairies and Sprites, even Pixies, as I realised I had had exposure to them as a child, albeit unknowingly, or at least unknowingly to me as an adult. But here I was sitting in the living room of the cottage and very much aware that there were Elementals in the fire. I sensed that there were quite a few of them. Then I heard, "*We are having so much fun just now! The strong wind means the flames lick up and we can slide and dance in them. We Salamanders are here to control and contain flames. Fire is the most destructive element on this planet. It is our job to ensure the planet's safety from it,*" the Salamander said.

This hitherto unseen world of nature's guardians was starting to unfold in front of me. Each element appears to have different types of guardians; plants have Fairies; animals have Pixies to act as protectors like we humans have Guardian Angels. Salamanders work with fire to protect against it getting out of control and destroying the other habitats. Since they were freely talking to me I started to think of questions to ask them. So I enquired, *"What about fires started by human carelessness?"* The response to this was, *"What we do in that situation is try to control it to the best of our abilities. This is not always easy, particularly when flammable materials are about. Please encourage people to be careful with their choice of fabrics and other furnishings for their homes. Education about fire safety is very important."*

By now I knew these were messages for my book and that was why they had made their presence known to me that evening. I thought to myself that I had better find out what Salamanders actually were. *"We live in the same dimension as Fairies however we are totally different beings. We are not healers; we are here to fulfill a protective role. Sometimes we are described as Fire Devas, however this is a misconception. Salamanders are Elementals in their own right. We protect from the destruction of fire but also use the destruction of fire for the good. Fire allows the renewal, the re-growth of an area. It may take many years but the energy of the area destroyed by the fire is cleansed,"* I was told. As a geographer I recognised the truth in this. Colonisation by new plants and creatures occur in the fire devastated areas.

It then occurred to me that fire was not a constant presence in the environment so I asked, *"Where do you go when there is no fire?"* The Salamander answered, *"Unlike Fairies we are not tied to a particular plant. We can flit from fire to fire within the vicinity. It is often different Salamanders in your fire each night. When you get a poor fire you blame the wood, however, it is more likely that the Salamanders don't like certain types of wood. It can be too hot for us so we dampen it down. When we do that however, the wood does not burn so well. The burning of the wood and how well it burns is dependent on the Salamanders' control. Man-made fibres and products have interfered with this however, which is why mammoth fires can occur and get out of control now and more people*

40

are killed due to noxious flames. This is a great concern for us as it means we are not able to play the protective role we wish to."

A Personal Message

The Salamander I was talking to continued, *"The balance on Earth is about to swing back to being more at one with nature and using natural products. We, along with other Elementals have been working hard, for the last twenty years especially, to get to this point. Many 'lightworkers'* (an esoteric term which refers to people engaged in raising the consciousness of humans) *who are incarnated Fairies and other etheric nature beings were sent to Earth to do this job."* His message then turned personal. *"You are one of them. You were sent because you possess the special gift of being able to talk to all of us, Angels, Archangels, Ascended Masters, Fairies and Elementals. Your job is to write this book and help open up this new age of awareness. Along with other lightworkers you will help protect Mother Earth and return her back to her natural glory."*

I knew of the new consciousness being brought in at the turn of the millennium. It was written about a lot in spiritual literature. I have always known that I wanted to protect our precious environment and its many inhabitants. I also knew from the time of my illness that I was a 'lightworker' as I am sure you are too. I knew it was part of my Divine path to write this book or why else would two powerful Archangels come and tell me this was what I had to do. I was quite excited by this message as it was direct confirmation of what I inherently knew. So I asked the Salamander, *"What else do you want me to know?"*

"We want you to know that we are here to help just like the Fairies but we are largely ignored in etherical literature. We would love you to put a drawing of us in your book!" was the reply I received. I laughed at this as art was my least favourite subject at school and I dropped it as soon as I could. The Salamander then said,

"*You need to work on your clairvoyance. When it opens you will be able to draw us or get someone else to.*" By now I was quite enjoying my chat with the Salamander. Richard was still away walking the dog so I started to think of what I thought were random questions to ask them for fun. I asked, "*Does a bigger flame have a bigger Salamander?*" The Salamander replied, "*Yes. We get bigger if we are trying to keep a bigger flame under control. Bonfires mean bigger Salamanders and thousands and thousands of little ones. Like Angels there is a Salamander hierarchy. For example, with the bush fires in Australia the Grande Salamanders are in charge of trying to control sections of the fire and they direct the smaller Salamanders.*"

It was only at this point that I realised I didn't know who the Salamander was talking to me. So I asked "*Are you a Grande Salamander?*" The answer was, "*No. I am your fire's guardian Salamander. Since you have an active coal fire I am in charge of calling in other Salamanders when you light your fire.*" This made me curious. Many countries use fire to cook on so I asked, "*In Africa where they cook on fires, how does that work?*" What I got told was, "*Well then, in that situation there is a guardian Salamander too, but it is not assigned to a fireplace but to the family or collective who light the fires. Your guardian Salamander will stay with the person, family or collective throughout the time they need fire. If they have no use for fire for years at a time and start using fire again a new guardian Salamander is sent. We are not like Guardian Angels.*"

Guardian Angels, in my understanding, are assigned to a soul to protect it through all incarnations. We all have Guardian Angels, who we can ask for help at any time because they are always with us. Once I started to speak to my Guardian Angel she was able to help me in many ways. The most important thing to remember is that we are never alone. A later chapter will discuss having Elementals as well as Angels as guardian etheric beings watching over us and keeping us safe. My mind went back to the Salamander saying I was a part incarnated Fairy. Although I was yet to learn what this really meant, as so much of this spiritual journey is truly a voyage of discovery, I then had the thought - I wonder if people can be incarnated Salamanders? *"Yes, however this can be problematic,"* the guardian Salamander said. *"More often than not the incarnated Salamander misses fire so much that it starts fires deliberately, particularly if they never have access to an open fire as a child. They may not even understand why they have a fascination with fire and many end up in prison."* This I found a sobering thought. Although it was fascinating how our souls all evolve and how different that makes us all. The fire was starting to die down now and so I thanked the Salamander for talking to me and he said, *"No problem. Come and talk to me again."*

Dragons Really Exist

I was quite excited about writing about Salamanders. I had originally thought I would just be writing about Fairies and Pixies but more Elementals were appearing to me. A couple of months after my first chat with the Salamander he told me that I needed more details about them and their link with Dragons for this book. Again I had read briefly about Dragon energy but had difficulty believing their existence and I had never really thought about them. I knew that the Goddess Pele was linked to active volcanoes and that lots of Salamanders and possibly Dragons would live in their fire so I called on Pele, the Hawaiian Goddess, and asked if she could help me. She came immediately and it was my first conversation with her. She said, *"I am glad you have at last called on me. One of my specialties is calling on fire Dragons and communing with them. The fire Dragons live in active volcanoes. They are probably the largest Elementals and certainly their energy is the most powerful. These creatures command great respect in the Devic Kingdom."*

The Devic Kingdom is otherwise known as the Elemental Realm. In some cultures the Elementals are referred to as the

Nature Devas. The Devic Kingdom includes not only Elementals, the beings who guard the Elements, but also the Nature Guardians such as Dragons, Unicorns and Mermaids. In this book we are only looking at the first level of the Devic Kingdom, the one that is closest to Earth, and is able to affect the physicality of the environment. As one moves up through the Devic Realm you will encounter the next layer of consciousness which is the home of the spirits referred to within eastern philosophies of China and Japan. Each river, each mountain, each ocean, glacier, volcano has a nature spirit this is also the guardian of that physicality. Pele continued, "*The Dragon's role is one of protection similar to the Salamander. You can call on a fire Dragon to protect you and your home if you are under psychic attack. In order to call on Dragon energy you need to be particularly advanced in your communications skills with Elementals. You also need to be pure in your intentions of their purpose. Earth Dragons also exist. There are not many left in the world nowadays but they tend to live in or underneath mountains. Earth Dragons are very good at healing disrupted earth energies and bringing energies of an area back into balance.*"

I was unaware until this moment that there were two types of Dragon and that each had different roles. At the time of writing this I have had no personal experience of contacting Dragons or using Dragon energy. Richard however, when he was in Wales doing some earth energy work was asked to free a trapped Dragon. There are lots of stories about Dragons being trapped in the middle ages through occult practices. Richard is not able to communicate clairaudiently with Dragons however he is very good at working with earth energies and etheric energy creations. To set the Dragon free from the spell that it was under he had to create and hand it a golden egg. This egg would break the curse placed on this Dragon; the only remaining Earth Dragon in the mainland of the United Kingdom at that time.

The Dragon is now free and happily living under/on its

mountain in Wales. I was told this by Saint Francis, the Ascended Master, when I asked one time if there were any Dragons living in the UK. I thought there might be some in Scotland but apparently not. If you are interested in Dragons, the Goddess Pele informs me that if you wish to commune or use Dragon energy for earth healing, you need to go through initiations before this can be done. It may be you were born with this gift having previously reached the required level or if this is an area that particularly interests you it is possible to take courses, to go through the initiation processes. The important thing to remember when communicating with Dragons is that they are probably the most powerful Elemental and any attempt to connect with them should be done with care.

Realisation

My life was starting to become rather extraordinary. I had known nothing of this Elemental world a few months prior and the reality of the many beings I had heard of only from mythology was being presented to me. If I hadn't had these experiences I am not sure I would have believed it. Yet something, somewhere deep inside me, within my soul recognised it all as the truth even if my logical brain tried to tell me otherwise. Probably the greatest lesson I have learned since my illness is that you should always listen to your heart and acknowledge your true feelings. My concerns that people would think I was mad were starting to disappear. The Salamander's message that I had come in as a soul to bring a new awareness and level of consciousness to people made me want to now fully embrace this gift and my spiritual life. Let it all truly begin, I now thought.

Appreciation & Invocation

Two Goddesses helped me with this chapter. Thank you to Goddess Pele who is a fire goddess and worshipped in Hawaii for her protection from fire and lava. To contact her she asked that you say:

"Powerful Goddess Pele, I call out to you now to help me in this time of change. Please help protect me and my home and keep us safe. Please help me to commune better with fire spirits, the Salamanders, so I can activate their protective power to keep me and my family safe. Thank you beautiful Pele."

I also need to thank the Goddess Vesta who is the Goddess of the hearth and home. Vesta's role is one in which she can bring family members closer together and create warmth within the relationships of the house. To contact her she asked that you said:

"Beautiful Vesta, Goddess of warmth. I call out to you today to ask you to help heal my relationship with (who or whatever it is). I ask for patience and courage when tackling this situation and I ask for your assistance in making my home a nicer and happy place to be for all who live in it. I ask you to help me see situations from a place of love and to loving act upon your guidance. Thank you for your kind assistance."

© Michele-lee Phelan

47

© Hayley Rust

Chapter 5
Woodland Guardians

It was three days after 'Hogmanay' (a Scottish term for New Year's Eve) and I was sitting in the living room of the cottage listening to some music. Romany was playing with his new blue ball that he had got for Christmas and was having great fun tossing it into the air and chasing it when it landed. Then, out of nowhere, a red admiral butterfly appeared flying above the dining table. I looked twice to be sure my eyes were not deceiving me, but there it was a butterfly in the house, quite alive, in the middle of winter! Richard had previously told me that butterflies hibernated in winter if they could find somewhere warm and safe enough. I had not known this fact and had always thought that they died at the end of summer. Evidently though the butterfly had been sleeping away in the corner of the house unnoticed, this was quite possible as the house had high ceilings and beams.

I watched the butterfly for a bit, mesmerised by it fluttering around the bookcase which had a vase of flowers on it, and a thought entered my head. Who looks after insects? As I have explained, I had very little knowledge of the different Elemental groups as I had only read one book on Fairies but it occurred to me that insects would have a nature guardian too. It is exciting when I meet a new nature guardian, so far having met Fairies, Pixies, Sprites, and Salamanders, it did occur to me that they just appear one day or I only become conscious of them at that moment. I had also been thinking about how many of the Elementals are written about in Scottish mythology. It intrigues me that our ancestors had previously had experiences with these creatures and that knowledge has been passed down in our folklore, yet today they are just considered as stories and myths.

The butterfly was now sitting on top of a flower in the vase so I asked, *"Who is your guardian Elemental?"* I heard a squeaky voice say, *"Imps."* It then explained, *"We Imps look after butterflies and all other insects. We are very small Fairies, tiny in comparison to humans. It is our job to safeguard the insect population. That means we live in communities with lots of other Elementals especially in woodland areas. As the insect guardians we are a key Elemental group because insects are a vital part of any ecosystem. As well as butterflies, Imps are the guardians of bees, spiders, caterpillars, beetles, slugs, snails and dragonflies to name a few. Bees and butterflies pollinate flowers and crops. Beetles and worms churn the earth to mix the vital bacteria and nutrients through the soil. Insects are a much undervalued member of the Animal Kingdom."*

The butterfly's Imp continued, "*Like Fairies we have the ability to help humans manifest their hopes and desires but few people call on us. We are often around when humans sit on the grass or walk through a meadow. We would like more people to try to commune with us. We are always excited to meet those who believe in us. We are particularly good at helping people who enjoy gardening and cut flower arranging. There are always insects in flowers and along with Fairies we help to keep flowers looking pretty and healthy and we want good homes for our insects."*

I thought this had been a lovely message the Imp had delivered to me. I felt a great deal of love for the Imp and I would say that Imps are one of my favourite Elementals. I seem to resonate well with their energy, by this I mean I enjoy being around them, like you do with your best friend for example. It then struck me that I had been an Imp! In the Brownies (organisation for girls) each Six (designated group or house within the organisation) is named after a different folklore creature such as Pixies, Kelpies and I had been in the Imps! This got me thinking well if Imps really exist, do Brownies?

The butterfly had now positioned itself on a different flower amongst the bunch so I thought I would ask the Imp what else it could tell me. It was as if the Imp could read my mind, which of course it could because Elementals can hear your thoughts and know your intentions and therefore can be communed with via thought alone. People often ask me, do you speak out loud to these beings? My reply is that I always speak out loud when I first talk to a new Elemental group but then just sometimes thereafter. I usually just think of the questions in my mind and then I can hear a reply.

The Imp replied to my thought by saying, *"Imps hope to ascend to the next level which is to be a Fairy or a Sprite. We have to practice being a nature guardian first, so often or not most Elementals start as an Imp or a Brownie. Brownies live in the woods and they do not have wings. They tend to look after non-flying insects such as centipedes and spiders but we Imps also help with their guardianship. Brownies are very small. At one time most of the earth was covered in forest and we all lived abundantly but as the forests diminished the numbers of Elementals did too. This is bad for the planet. Part of the magic of the world is our presence. We hope those people who read your book will help to stop the deforestation that is occurring at an alarming rate in the world in whatever way they can."* I had now discovered that each Elemental group has given an environmental warning to me without me asking directly for one in most cases. They have all given guidance as to what we can do to help which is encouraging and I hope everyone reading this will do what they can to assist them in the protection of the environment. The Imp finished our chat that evening by saying, *"Bringing Elementals into your world will trigger remembrance in your brains of magic that you all once had within you."*

I have had various chats with Imps since and each time the Imps have wished to have extra bits added into a certain chapter by them. One evening I was speaking on the phone to Richard and he said there was a lace wing flying about in the lamp shade. Again it was an unusual time of the year for this insect to be about. I said to him, *"Maybe it has come so you can try to talk to it."* He has been asking his Guardian Angels to help him to develop his clairaudience and been trying to manifest this with the Fairies. Two nights later we were on the phone and again a lace wing appeared flying inside the lampshade.

This time I had a strong feeling it was appearing so Richard could talk to its Imp. He tried to talk to it but could not hear any reply. Then I heard, as if I was sitting there in the room, a squeaky voice say *"Imps are the easiest Elemental group to commune with first. We have more patience than Fairies in this respect. Keep trying, you will hear us one day."* So my advice is if you are currently trying to commune with Fairies or Elementals in general and you see an insect, ask its Imp to talk to you. You might just hear a little squeaky voice talking back!

More Elemental Groups

I was thinking one day about my first Imp chat and about what it had said. It said that Imps were an important part of the woodland environment and I wondered what other Elementals lived in the woods next to our house in the Borders. As I had that thought my Guardian Angel, Sophia, started speaking to me. She started telling me about Wood Nymphs, Elves and Gnomes! *"Wood nymphs are small etheric beings similar to Elves but smaller. They look after tree dwelling creatures for example squirrels, tree creepers, and ants. Although each creature has a specific Elemental guardian group, Wood Nymphs are assigned to the tree rather than the animal. They look like small little boys often dangling from the twigs of a tree,"* she explained.

"Elves don't live on the branches of the trees like Wood Nymphs. The Elves live in the undergrowth often around the roots of the trees and bushes. Elves roles are to protect the undergrowth, along with Gnomes who live on the ground. Elves are small with no wings. They aspire to become Gnomes. The Gnomes resonate with Earth energies. They are often protectors of ley lines and Earth energy centres. They are not Elementals who are healers like Fairies

and Sprites. It is however possible to commune with Gnomes but they tend to be grumpy. There are lots of Gnomes in the woods near the cottage. This is what attracts Romany into the forest," she continued. This made Richard and myself laugh out loud. I was relaying the message to him as I was receiving it.

Romany gets walked every night round the forest but there is a bit he always disappears into for a good five minutes. Richard had previously remarked upon this and said it looked like he was chasing something in the forest that he couldn't see. So I had asked Romany one time what it was he was doing at this point in his nightly walks. By now Romany's higher self would answer my questions quite freely. He said sheepishly "*I know I am not meant to chase the Gnomes who live in the forest but they are so stupid sometimes. I find it great fun playing with them. They are scared of me because I chase them and they all run away but can't move that fast.*" He added quickly, "*I don't hurt them though ever. It is just play.*"

Sophia's message then turned more pressing. "*Try to teach him not to chase them as he distracts them from the job they are there to do. There are lots of ley lines up the hills round about where you live and the Gnomes are there to harness the energy and put it into the earth. The Gnome is often portrayed as a stupid creature in myth but this is because they cannot fly and have small short dumpy legs. They are wise creatures however and what they can impart to you will be significant. Just keep Romany away when you want to talk to them!*" I made a mental note to heed Sophia's advice when the time came.

Wood Nymph And Elves

A month and a half later I still hadn't yet spoken to a Gnome or a Wood Nymph. I set off walking into the wood beside the house with the dog in tow. I tied Romany up to one of the trees and headed towards my favourite pine tree. I like this tree because its trunk is bent. It looks like it started to grow at a forty-five degree angle and then thought it had better straighten it-self up! It has beautiful big bough branches which I crept underneath and I could then stand upright beside its trunk. It felt like the tree was protecting me underneath its great arms. Out of the corner of my etherical eye I detected movement. Of course I looked with my physical eyes when I turned and could see nothing on the branch, but I could feel I was being watched by more than one pair of eyes. So I asked whoever it was that was there to talk to me.

I heard a young male voice say, *"We are Wood Nymphs."* I said, *"Hello,"* and asked them how they were. The Wood Nymph said, *"Very well, how are you?"* They were very polite Elementals! I couldn't really see them so I asked what they were wearing. I got told they wore flat hats, trousers to just below the knee and long sleeved tunic tops. I could then see one sitting on the edge of the branch dangling his legs. I asked if he liked living on this tree. He said, *"Yes, we were invited to live here."* I thought that was odd so I asked what he meant. He said, *"The Tree Spirit asks the Nymphs to join his tree, tend to his branches and look after the creatures that live on them. Wood nymphs must be invited to reside in a tree; therefore we can't choose our homes."* I discovered from this that Elementals have etiquette they have to adhere to! I also found out about a new Elemental - the Tree Spirit.

I now had an understanding of why I find woodlands very magical places to be in. There are so many different types of Elementals residing within them. It started to rain so I thanked the Wood Nymph for our chat and I moved out from underneath the tree knowing I had to speak to Tree Spirits. I walked away from the Pine tree thinking I will wait till Spring and I headed off back to the house. The rain was not heavy but I had to cross a grass meadow which bracken was now encroaching onto. Bracken is an introduced species that suffocates the undergrowth, stopping all the other plants from growing. My sixth sense seemed particularly heightened that day. I was sure there were presences making themselves known to me in the roots of the dead bracken and I decided to stop and see who it was. To my delight when I asked I was told it was some Elves! Again I could not see them but I could feel and hear them. Romany had noticed too as he was standing motionless staring at the same spot I was.

The Elf said to me, *"We Elves love the rain. It is the best thing to energetically purify the undergrowth, of which we are guardians. Elves' jobs are to tend to the plants and trees. The roots are of vital importance to the soil ecosystems of the planet. Roots are not only soil stabilisers but also ensure water intake to the plant or tree and nutrient supply. Elves are a bit like Wood Nymphs in that we have no set thing to guard. We work with Gnomes a lot but it is not our job to fix earth energy. Elves also work with Fairies to help protect a plant. The Fairies tend to the flower, while the Elves tend to the roots,"* he explained. That made sense I thought and fascinating that they should work as part of a team. The Elf continued, *"The ecosystems of the soils are being depleted greatly however because of intensive farming which is stripping the soils of nutrients. Pollutant fallout from the air and chemicals sprayed on the fields affect the shrubs and trees all around,"* he said sadly.

The environmental messages, from the Nature Guardians were becoming clearer. Our lifestyles are impacting immensely on nature. Something I had known and believed for a long time. When I went to University in 1998 there was still mixed belief in the scientific community as to whether humans were causing global warming. Now nearly ten years on the evidence is overwhelming. Were the Elementals providing me with warnings for the state of the soils for the future? I believed so. I was now really keen as an environmentalist to find out from the Nature Guardians what wisdom they could impart. My journey now shifted from curiosity about this other realm and the job they do in safeguarding the planet, to the environmental knowledge they could pass to me.

Appreciation & Invocation

Thank you to Goddess Cordelia who helped me with this chapter. Cordelia is a Celtic Irish Goddess whose mission is to help those willing to protect nature. She is a close guardian of the Wood Nymphs and Elves she has explained to me. Her job is to encourage people into nature. To invoke Cordelia to assist you, she asked that you say:

"Cordelia I call out to you now to help protect and guide me. I wish to enhance my environment and help heal and protect my local trees, bushes and woodland. Please Cordelia give me a mission to help do this and to make my world a better and enhanced habitat to reside in. Help me to notice nature more and see the beauty in all the Divine's creation. Thank you Cordelia for your support."

© Jane Starr Weils

© Hayley Rust

Chapter 6
Air Spirits In Crisis

The climate is of great importance as is the air that we breathe because air is fundamental to all life. The composition our air unique in our solar system and is what allows life, as we know it, to be sustained. Within the atmosphere, systems and structures are constantly at work. The atmosphere and the oceans are closely linked; as a feedback mechanism with one another, the ocean temperatures, for example, give rise to cloud formation and the wind speeds generate waves. Yet even more complex feedback loops and mechanisms occur, many of which scientists are just discovering. The issue of global warming is widely acknowledged and recognised by scientists and politicians as posing the greatest global threat to life on Earth. I knew that the main message of this book was the about the vital role Elementals play in the upkeep of planet Earth. With the issue of global warming on the news nearly everyday in some form; extensive flooding, forest fires, malaria carrying mosquitoes being found in England, I set about finding an Air Elemental. I decided to ask Maeve for guidance. She informed me that there were Air Elementals; the most commonly known ones were a group called Sylphs. They are the Wind Guardians and are hard to contact because they are constantly on the move. She would arrange for me to have a chat with one.

A few days later Maeve told me it was time to have my Sylph chat. It didn't surprise me that my Sylph chat was inside; the house was extremely drafty and had open fires. Richard grabbed his notebook and started to write the Sylph's message that I relayed. I was unable to see the Sylph but I could clearly hear her. Elementals, like humans, all have different voices a bit like our regional dialects. You can tell when you are talking to a different group, just the same as you could tell a 'Glaswegian' from a 'Liverpudlian'. The Sylph said, *"We Sylphs float through air on currents of wind never residing anywhere except wind. Our role is one of cleaning for as much as we enjoy life our aim is to purify the air. Unfortunately we are overwhelmed these days by the vast amounts of pollution you humans are putting into the air. Vast factories churn out chemicals that strip us of our magical powers and are hindering us in the cleaning up job we are trying to do."*

The Sylph mentioning her magical power made me recall that all the other Elementals had alluded to or directly referred to these abilities. I questioned what magic means in our language. So I looked in a Collins dictionary. It defined magic as 'any mysterious or extraordinary quality or power'. It seemed to explain what the Elementals were saying; a power that they have that is not in our comprehension of the physical world. I think the word 'magic' was developed to explain the 'inexplicable' at that time. For example, 'hand healing' techniques such as Reiki, are an accepted technique today but would have once been described as 'using magic'. Yet Reiki is a human way of harnessing the healing power of the universe and channelling it in a specific direction. This is an example of humans using the universal energies in the same way that the Fairies and Sylphs are describing as their magical abilities. Realising the Elementals are blessed with these special gifts in order to create such beauty to keep the energy of Earth clean thus allowing us, the animals and plants to thrive during our lifetime, I think it is quite disrespectful of us not to care about our actions and how they are impacting on the lives of the Elementals.

The Sylph continued her message, *"The chlorofluorocarbons (CFCs) that were pumped out into the atmosphere in the 1980s were a major destructive force against planet Earth. Thousands and thousands of Sylphs were injured in process."* Horror struck me at this point. I had studied the effects of CFCs and the creation of the hole in the ozone layer around the planet while at University. The ozone layer's role is to filter out the sun's harmful ultra violet rays which otherwise would penetrate Earth and its inhabitants. The ozone hole that was discovered over Antarctica is thought to have been the cause of increased skin cancer statistics as well as being a cause of the melting ice sheets. To think that these chemicals (found in aerosols and refrigerators) had also injured thousands of Elementals made me incredibly upset. The chemical industry has manufactured poisons that are destroying the balance of this glorious planet and all her intricate and purposeful checks and balances. At least now the world is waking up to this, albeit slowly. The Sylph went on to explain their role, *"Our role was meant to keep the atmospheric gases in balance and harmony with the cycles due to occur on Earth, as part of the natural oscillations. However with the burning of fossil fuels our role became increasingly difficult. There are not enough Sylphs to keep up with the cleaning process. Pollutants can travel thousands of miles and we have to clean up the air from pollution that is very widespread. We are an Elemental group that is currently under much stress at this time. Any assistance and prayers intended towards the Sylphs would be gratefully received."*

Their Homes

I made a mental note to send prayers regularly to the Sylphs when I could. This was a very disturbing message. It was the first Elemental group that truly seemed to be saying they were in crisis. Our habits and lifestyles are now impacting too much on their roles of protecting and safeguarding the air. I was puzzled however by where Sylphs lived. All the Elementals I had met so far had resided in a particular part of Scotland, but wind was everywhere, so I asked, *"Are you resident in the same area?"* The Sylph replied, *"No we blow wherever the wind takes us. We stay in the current. There are many hundreds of thousands of us out at sea."* So I now knew that they lived in the wind but what if there was no wind, was it air they lived in or just wind currents? *"In the air, however we can move more freely in the wind."* she replied. I was still puzzled as to how they purified the air. The Sylph explained, *"We purify the air using the energetic force of the kinetic* energy of the wind currents. We, like Fairies, have magical skills and powers to dissolve non man-made chemicals, but no powers against CFCs because they are a man-made product. We have no skills to counteract that, especially the vast volumes at which these chemicals were becoming airborne. It is not the current of the wind that is blowing away the pollution, it is us. We do not tackle the particles that cause colouration, nor do we remove smell it is not our jobs. Our job is as a gas regulator."

Air is made up of gases that vary from place to place and at different times. Nitrogen and oxygen make up nearly ninety per cent of clean air. However water vapour, dust particles and ozone are also present and have significant effects on the climate even although they are only present in small quantities. These are some of the non man-made gases and chemicals the Sylphs are equipped to deal with. Carbon dioxides, nitrogen oxide, sulphur dioxide and particulates occur naturally in small numbers also, however since the industrial revolution and the advent of burning fossil fuels through transportation and industrial processes they are present in the atmosphere in much larger quantities. It is this, and the advent of new airborne chemicals, that the Sylphs are struggling with. Air pollution has become a big environmental and political issue since the 1980s. I had studied it in great depth during my degree, but as a scientist, nature spirits had never entered the equation.

I was curious now to find out what Sylphs looked like. I asked her to describe herself. She said, "Sylphs are feminine, we have long hair down to our feet, of similar size to a Fairy except we are elongated and bendy. We glide in the wind." With my third eye, I then saw a beautiful, small Sylph appear before me. She looked at me and I asked her if she interacted with other Elementals? "Elementals always interact. We all work as part of a team although the Sylphs are probably the most independent because we never stop. We fly at great speeds in flocks of hundreds. Our healing role for the planet is one of cleaning. We do not work on healing plants, trees, animals or humans. We have no power to stop the destructive force of wind, we are not wind controllers just wind's passengers." I had a glorious image of a gust of wind carrying these mesmerising little Elementals along, as if they were sailing to their next destination, their hair streaming behind them. She brought my attention back to her by saying, *"It is a good life being a Sylph. I would not swap it for the world. My main message is 'stop polluting the air'. Think about what you are burning, is that car trip really necessary? Could I walk or cycle? Do I need to take that flight or could I go by train? Think about the consequences of your decisions for the planet as a whole. If everybody would just think, the world would be in a better state. Think how it feels to sit on top of a hillside with the sun on your face, wind on your cheeks, air smelling fresh and pure. We wish that cleanliness and exhilarated sense could be experienced by all every moment of every second of every day! That is how the world should be."*

It was evident that the impact on the atmosphere by the human race is huge. Yet at the same time the Sylphs bore no grudge and wished to create the best environment for those living on earth. I wondered how long Sylphs live for. It was a question I had not thought to ask the other Elemental groups I had met. The Sylph explained to me that they were one of the longest living Elementals because their role is not cyclically dependent but in a way an Elemental never dies. None of us truly do though I thought; we just go home. Our physical bodies die but our souls return to spirit world. The Sylph then explained what happens to Elementals, *"We can elevate or we can lose our magical powers and then can no longer do work on earth. It is the same for all Elementals however when an Elemental becomes traumatised energetic blockage occurs."* It dawned on me that if air pollution can block the Sylphs energetically we must be doing the same thing to all the Elementals. If I were to ask you to list all the types of environmental pollution you could think of that we as a race are causing on the planet, I am sure you would struggle to name an environment that we are not impacting on, directly or indirectly. It had been a long chat with the Sylph and I could sense she wanted to return to her wind and join her fellow Sylphs. I enjoyed my conversation. It was stimulating because she had introduced concepts that I had not considered before.

Pan's Visit

After the Sylph left I thought my work was done for the evening. However, a couple of hours later I became aware of a very powerful spiritual being. It was the change in energy that caught my attention. This energy was different to any Angel, Ascended Master or Goddess that I had spoken too. It was much more powerful than any Elemental I had met. The energy was not threatening; it was just different to anything I had experienced. I asked who our guest was. To my utter surprise and delight, my Guardian Angel said it was Pan. I had heard of Pan, the Great Greek God of the Environment but that was all I knew. He is usually depicted in legend as half goat, half man. I knew little else about him. His energy felt amazing, encompassing the whole room. His power and warmth was infiltrating every nook and cranny making my hairs tingle throughout my body. It was as if my soul was connecting with a power so great yet so familiar at the same time. I felt a lot of strength within my body again, a sensation I had not experienced since the illness. Pan was surveying me. I doubted he was interested in my hair and clothing, so I figured he must have been looking at my spiritual qualities, perhaps even measuring my soul. It was a strange experience and one I have not had again. It was awesome, that such a great deity had come to find me and was allowing me to be in his presence. I decided to introduce myself.

Pan spoke in a very commanding voice, *"There are Elemental beings in the clouds. Few people have written about them. They are called Sylphons and they are in charge of cloud formation, regulating rainfall, and helping manage weather conditions. They control the monsoons and droughts. They work with other Elementals to control the climate cycles that the Earth is dependent on. The Sylphons dictate the cloud formation in order to balance the cyclical climate on Earth.*

64

Their role is also very affected by global warming and man-made climate change. They work in tandem with the other Elementals to bring snow, hail and rain when required. This was all previously done through natural oscillations of the Earth, however it's been hampered by the climate change. The Sylphons regulatory roles are difficult. They are struggling with containing destructive weather forces such as tornadoes and hurricanes which are a type of cloud formation. They ensure hurricanes only occur when the energy of that area needs it for energy clearing. Scientists find hurricanes and tornadoes occur on energetic hotspots and these require cleaning and regulation. As the temperature rises new levels unprecedented are being reached in the force of these storms." I scribbled down his words verbatim. It was always predicted by scientists that storms would increase in intensity and frequency with global warming. I understood what Pan was saying but thoughts were going through my head about the loss of life, not just human but animal and plant too, that these storms could cause. Curious as I was about the Sylphons, it was Pan at this moment that I wanted to know more about. So I asked him about himself. *"I am the Great God Pan. I have the legs of a goat and the torso of a man. My role on this planet is to oversee the Elementals. It is my job to make sure they are all informed of any changes and I work in tandem with Gaia and Geb to keep the planet in homeostasis at this time of great turmoil. My role is vital and involves communicating the changes Gaia requires to keep all her systems in balance,"* he informed me.

For those unfamiliar with Gaia, she is also known as Mother Earth. In the 1980s an independent research scientist, James Lovelock proposed a theory that Earth was a living, breathing entity called Gaia and that she was in charge of all the natural systems that occurred on planet earth. In Greek mythology Gaia was believed to be the Earth Goddess and the Earth was worshipped by many other ancient cultures as a deity. Geb represents the masculine energy of Gaia. Egyptian mythology defines Geb as the male representation of the physical plane, God of the earth; father of Osiris and Isis. Pan continued his message,

"One of the major areas of change is for the work of the Sylphons. Their main role is that of formation of clouds and mist. They were previously guided by the atmospheric changes and temperature to trigger them to form clouds. This has however, in the last fifty years, become increasing difficult for them to predict. Now I have to give them messages direct from Gaia; her requirements to keep her atmosphere and ocean systems under control. This is a major change for the Sylphons. They are struggling greatly hence more erratic weather patterns are forming."

Pan had evidently read my previous thoughts and continued, "People may wonder why they are choosing to form such massive hurricanes and tornadoes and why some areas are being starved of rain. We are loathed to form such acts of destruction but it is at the moment the only way to keep the planet and Gaia's system in some kind of balance. Air pollution is a worldwide issue. The atmospheric system is the more important feeder to all the other systems. Air traffic pollution is taking up so much of the Sylphs' and Sylphons' time, trying to purify the effects of it, they are under the greatest stress. Of all the Elementals their plight is the worst." I was hit by a wave of sadness for the Air Spirits. Air travel has increased dramatically over the last twenty years but at what cost? What legacy were we going to leave to our future generations? I thanked Pan for visiting me. I felt he would be back. The situation of the Air Spirits seemed very bad. I went to bed wondering what could be done. Air is fundamental to life; crucial to the survival of our planet.

Appreciation & Invocation

Thank you to the Great God Pan for his help and guidance with this chapter. If you wish to work with and invoke Pan he asked that you say:

"Great God Pan, come to my side now please. Explain to me the situation with the Earth at this time and what can be done. Please guide me in my actions and help me to make changes to my lifestyle. Please show me the way to improving the Air Spirits plight and the environment I live in general. Thank you for your help Pan."

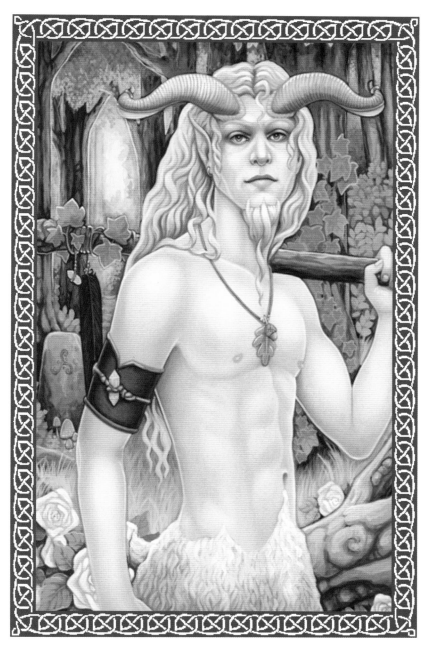

© Michele-lee Phelan

67

© Judy Mastrangelo

68

Chapter 7
Maeve's Message

The Air Spirits messages had been greatly concerning. The scale of the problem was so huge I was at a loss to see what I could do to help them. The problem of global warming and the reduction of carbon dioxide in the atmosphere seemed so colossal. World climate summits were being held by top scientists and political leaders trying to find a solution and ways of tackling the problem. As an individual who cares passionately about the planet I was perplexed as to what I individually could do.

Then one day as I was sitting staring out the cottage window, looking at the tree tops blanketing the valley down below, Maeve appeared by my side. I couldn't see her; she has only shown herself to me once, but I could feel her presence. Maeve has a very gentle energy, very attuned with the Fairy energy I have felt when communicating with Fairies, except hers is much more powerful. We began to chat. I speak to Maeve as if she is my sister, so familiar I am now with her presence in my life. As I have said before she is one of my guides while I write this book.

Maeve asked me that day if she could have a chapter in my book her to convey her message directly to the reader. She told me she wanted to teach readers about the Fairies' powers of manifestation. I agreed and grabbed my notebook, excited to hear what she had to say. She asked me to explain that her role as such is to oversee the Fairy Kingdom and to ensure the Fairies are carrying out their roles for the protection of the planet. She is their spiritual leader, giving them guidance and assistance when they ask. Maeve, like other Goddesses, Ascended Masters and Archangels, can be at different places throughout the world at the same time. This is possible because she lives in a higher dimension than the Fairies and other Elementals, and higher than the dimension human beings and animals live in. Goddesses, like Angels, are not constricted by time or space in the way humans are. For those of you unfamiliar with Angels, and I am aware I have mentioned them a lot so far, they are the divine beings that guide and protect us humans. They are messengers from God (the Divine) and their job is to guide us through our life path and keep us safe. They are unable to interfere in our lives unless we directly ask them to, however they will directly interfere unasked if we are in a life threatening situation before our time, perhaps one explanation for remarkable escapes and near death experiences. Angels are beings of pure love as are the Goddesses, who as well as having specific areas of expertise, are always available to help humans who call upon them for their assistance in life.

Maeve asked me to inform you that you should never worry about calling on her to help you any time you require her assistance because she can be working with the Fairies and communing with you at the same time. Maeve, like all Fairies, is a powerful manifestor. By this she means she can help you to manifest (make happen) whatever you wish as long as it is Divine accordance for her to do so. Maeve is particularly good at helping humans who believe in Divine magic, work with animals (protecting and caring for) and those who wish to look after and take better care of the environment. She is especially helpful in situations where conflict is resulting in environmental damage. She can be called upon if you are worried about the environment of a war-torn area or an area where testing of nuclear weapons is occurring, for example. All the Elementals in this area will be grateful for your prayers and the added strength you give them to deal with the after effects of the war or disaster. This is the same for natural disasters too.

Maeve explained that she has a special affection for children and women and will help any mother who calls on her to help heal her child or her relationship with the child. She said she has very powerful healing powers for all living things and will work with healers of all kinds. When called on, her beautiful energy can envelop any troubling situation and smooth it out resolving in a harmonious outcome. She is especially gentle in sensitive situations and her loving, soothing energy can work behind the scenes to bring resolutions of troubling situations and conflict especially when it appears as if all else has failed. Like working with all Goddesses, Ascended Masters, Angels and Elementals all we humans have to do is release our troubles over to them and trust that they will heal the situation for the best; often with outcomes that are beyond our wildest dreams.

Maeve then gave me a direct message for the readers of this book. Let her wise words of wisdom sink into you as you read her text for hidden in the wording and tone of her speech are encoded patterns which your unconscious mind will pick up even if your conscious mind is unaware. *"I call upon all lightworkers reading this book to start work on your Divine mission. You have been sent to Earth to do a job and by reading this book you are awakening to your calling. When souls incarnate as humans we often forget the job we agreed to do on Earth. We are often sidetracked by the many material delights this great world has to offer.*

How many of you reading this think there is something missing in your life? How many think your job or career is not as rewarding as you thought it would be or not as enjoyable as it once was? How many of you feel there is a part of you itching to break out of your situation, to do something totally different? Something new; something you had not considered before? You are being called now to start to do the job you as a soul were sent to do.

Some of you will be healers, here to care for others, to study homeopathy or herbal medicine to heal in a more holistic, chemical-free approach. Others will find their call in the arts; to do music therapy, paint, sing, act to bring enjoyment and the healing gift of laughter to the world. Others among you will have been sent to heal and protect the environment, to work with the Elementals, to bring a better harmony and balance back to Mother Earth. It is important that what inner urges you feel reading the above, that you acknowledge the stirring and awakening of your true self. It is its way of crying out to you to read more, and participate more in whatever interests and excites you. Many lightworkers feel relief when they start work on their Divine mission, they often feel their life has slotted into place and great joy and happiness has entered their lives. Many find and meet their true love, who they have been searching for all their life, but had been looking in the wrong place.

The Elementals, especially Fairies, are very adept at helping people find their true love. Just ask the Fairies to help you manifest whatever you wish for in a partner. But be careful what you wish for! Think long and hard about what you truly want from a partner before you put it on your list. The Fairies will also help heal any blocks you have to giving and receiving true love. Go sit in your favourite nature spot, perhaps it is somewhere you know or feel Fairies and other Elementals exist. Just get comfortable, relax, open your heart to feel love and ask the Fairies to help you with whatever your problem is. Ask to be healed of any blocks in your life that are stopping you from experiencing true love. Be open to receiving help.

If you like try to mentally commune with the Fairies, those of you who are clairaudient will be able to hear their replies, those of you who are not, ask to be shown a sign. The Fairies are delighted when asked to help. It is a good idea to sleep with a leafed plant beside your bed that way the Fairies can work on you while you sleep plucking out any negative energy you picked up during the day. You can also ask the Fairies to enter your dreams at night to show you answers to questions you may have asked them during the day.

Fairies are particularly helpful if you have a passion for the environment. If you wish to welcome Fairies into your life, start to pay attention to your habits and see if there is a more environmentally friendly way of doing things. When you welcome Fairies into your lives you will notice the abundance of gifts they shower on you grateful humans. It may be you noticing and smelling a beautiful flower. It may be a feather floating in the wind, or a ray of sunshine hitting the top of a mountain or perhaps a fish jumping out of a stream. These are all gifts the Divine Creator has bestowed on us.

The more you begin to work with Fairies, the more in harmony with the Earth and her cycles you will become. The seasons of the earth are the most obvious cycle to you humans. Spring is the time of regrowth, renewal and regeneration, Summer is the culmination of the energy and growth produced in Spring. Autumn is the time to reap the rewards of harvest, and the onset of decay. Winter is the down period where hibernation occurs and systems conserve energy ready to burst into action again in the Spring.

There are other cycles which affect humans on Earth but many rarely notice or appreciate its powers: the Moon. Moon cycles have a great impact for life on earth. It is not just the tides that are affected by the gravitational pull of the moon. Fairies and Elementals work in tandem with the moon. There are thirteen moon cycles a year. The waxing moon means the moon is getting bigger. This is the time the Fairies start working on the healing of their plant. They heal continuously but it is at the time of the waxing moon that their healing powers are greater. The Fairies use the moon cycles as their guide to maximise the energy available on Earth for healing. The full moon, or just before it, is the time to get rid of the old or anything that is not working. It is the time to best utilise the energies for change. The full moon is the time to recharge, cleanse healing instruments, and in the Fairies case, to take a moon bath. Humans can benefit too by sitting out on a clear night and bathing in the healing rays of the full moon (the time it is most powerful on earth).

Just as the moon starts to wane is the ideal time to manifest your hopes and desires. The Fairies are experts at manifestation so call on them at this time to help you fulfill your manifestation list. Energy needs to be put in by yourself as well as your Fairy helpers to make this happen. When you manifest events are changed to make things happen. It is important to just go with the flow and not analyse or judge things. Then they can fall into place. Humans when they incarnate often forget that the gift of manifestation is within, within every single one of you. As humans your thoughts are a manifestation tool so the secret to manifestation is to think as if you already have what you are wanting. Visualise how it will be and how it will feel. This is manifestation. This is why if you think negatively or fear something you can actually find that situation occurring, because you have manifested it!

Through my message in this book, I wish to convey to everyone reading this, that healing and manifestation is within you all. You all have the power and equal right to use your spiritual gifts. These gifts do not just have to be used for work on yourself but can be used to heal others and the planet. The Elementals in areas of pollution or desiccation due to natural disasters often are struggling to do their work because their healing powers have been reduced. So it is important you know that by just thinking of an area and its Elementals with love, and sending them love you are healing that area. The Elementals will be grateful for your help. The more you work with them, the more joy will enter your life and the easier life will become. I congratulate you for taking the time to read this book and to awaken a lost part within your soul. May many blessings come your way."

Appreciation & Invocation

Thank you to Maeve for her help and guidance with this chapter. If you wish to show your appreciation, have her work with you then invoke Maeve by saying:

"Dear Maeve, please help me awaken onto my divine path. Please show me what it is I am meant to do. Help me to reconnect to the rhythms of the earth and so use them to access my full manifestation potential. Thank you for helping me make my dreams come true."

© Judy Mastrangelo

75

© Judy Mastrangelo

Chapter 8
Mystery Of The Birds

Maeve has helped me a lot in my recovery by teaching me new ways to look at situations. She has guided me in where to go to have the experiences I have had. My recovery was steadily continuing, I could walk further, was gradually getting stronger and was no longer constantly tired. I had lost the fear that grips you in recovery from an illness which requires such cautious rehabilitation; that a relapse may occur at any time. I was starting to feel confident again about life, about trying new things and I was enjoying success in new achievements. I was also starting to see a path, not only in my recovery but in my spiritual development leading clearly in front of me too. It felt good to have got to this point.

I wondered why I had never read any books or magazines on spirituality before, because I was enjoying it so much now. I have read that often people go through 'wake-up calls' to get them onto their divine path and I am glad that this had happened to me at a relatively young age even though at the time it was scary and utter hell to live through. Life now was so much richer and exciting. I no longer cared what people thought of what I was doing. The more I understood about the Elemental realm the more it made sense to me.

Many times in the past I had made judgements of people which I see now I had no right to do. We each have our own path to follow and our own experiences to endure. When I had taken ill I was only three months into my dream job. I had just started to work for RSPB Scotland as their Conservation Policy Officer in Edinburgh. My job was to lobby government and get better policies to protect wetland and farmland birds. I felt it was so unfair initially that I fell so ill doing this job that I had always wanted to do. But I realise now that although it was what I wanted to do at the time, when something is taken away from you it is often replaced with something better.

I wanted to work for the RSPB so much because of my love for birds. They mesmerise me. Their beaks, their legs, their wings and most of all their feathers hold a fascination for me. I can sit for hours watching them feeding, fighting for territory and preening. During the time when I was trapped in the one room, my walls were adorned with paintings of birds; Toucan, Penguin, Falcon, Kestrel, a family of Ducks and postcards of Budgies. You see, I love the energy of birds; the way garden birds flit from branch to branch, knock each other off a feeder and hop along the ground, yet in the sky they are so graceful. In Perthshire where I grew up, I took the regular sight of birds of prey such as Sparrow Hawks and Ospreys for granted.

I believe that in the bird, we see one of the most spiritual creations and that is why, especially in Scotland, we are one of the most bird loving countries. They exist in such numbers and variations, reminding us often daily, of our connection as souls to the Divine Creator. The myths and folklore surrounding birds interest me greatly.

Who Guards Birds?

The birds aided me a lot in my recovery, watching them helped pass endless hours especially when I could not yet read, write or watch television. To occupy myself I would often watch the antics of the blackbirds in the garden. The blackbird is regarded in Celtic mythology as a spiritual awakener. Superstition still exists today, for example, the sighting of only one magpie is meant to signify bad luck.

A few years ago a blackbird started visiting our garden. This female blackbird was unable to hop properly and could therefore not scrat for food. Outside my parents' kitchen window is a wooden fence which she would often sit on, so we started to feed her sultanas out the window. The other blackbirds however cottoned on and would come too. When

I would open the kitchen curtains there would be a row of blackbirds sitting on the fence waiting for their raisins. Some would get bold and fly to the window sill. Some would become even bolder and hop in the open window in the summer, much to the annoyance of my mother who would have to clean up the mess from their panic to get back out!

One day I was in the kitchen boiling the kettle. It was the middle of January, the sky was clear, but it was still bitterly cold. I looked out the window and saw a blackbird sitting on the fence intently staring at me. It had been six months since a blackbird had sat there waiting for raisins. I had been thinking just the day before about which Elemental I would meet next. I silently asked who was this blackbird's guardian and I heard 'Fairy'. I thought that can't be right, Fairies look after plants, but I knew the birds had different Elemental guardians depending on their type because I had already been told that water birds had Sprites. The blackbird flew away as if it had completed its task and I wondered which Goddess or Ascended Master I could talk to about birds.

Then Saint Francis appeared to me. I had spoken to him before and of course he is the Patron Saint of birds. He told me that garden birds more often than not had Fairies as their guardians. He then expanded, *"The bird is a magnificent creature. The diversity of size, colour and habitat dwelling means there are always some around humans regardless of location. The plumage, colour and the bird song have held a fascination for humans from the beginning of your creation. The bird, of all creatures defines spiritual purity. With their grace of flight, the sweetness of their call and the beauty of their feathers, birds are like sparkles of Divine light fluttering around peoples' lives. Unlike animals, birds have different primary Elemental guardians depending on the environment they live in. Water birds have Sprites as their own guardians. Garden birds, parakeets and farmland birds have Fairies. Raptors, vultures and other birds of prey have Pixies. Ground dwelling birds which cannot fly tend to have Gnomes or Elves as their guardian."* I thought 'wow'; birds are very unique in this respect.

All the Elementals he mentioned I had met as guardians of other groups. Yet all the other groups seemed to just have the one primary type of guardian regardless of species. St. Francis continued, *"You must now go and meet parakeets and penguins and hear their story. Birds are often very wise. They bring lots of magical energy into people's lives."* No surprise that the largest charity in the UK is the RSPB, Royal Society for the Protection of Birds. As an organisation, it was a very important and influential environmental lobby group. At that time I knew that protecting birds was important but I had no idea of the spiritual importance of them for the planet.

St. Francis added to my thoughts, *"Few people are aware why birds are so special. They are very sensitive creatures and need to be protected from the damage that humans are doing to the planet. A lot of their habitats are in danger from deforestation and loss of hedgerows, wetlands and other changes such as climate and also from herbicides sprayed on fields killing their food. The Fairies that protect birds are very concerned about climate change. This is greatly affecting migrations and potentially, food supply. The chemicals that are sprayed on the fields affect the birds' fertility in some species resulting in smaller broods. Other species are going extinct especially some species of parrot due to the loss of habitat. The Fairies urge you to protect our birds and campaign against rainforest destruction. Birds are a very important part of the ecosystem of the planet."*

I enjoyed my chat that day with Saint Francis. He had said I needed to speak to penguins. Obviously no penguins live in the wilds of Scotland however I knew that Edinburgh Zoo had the largest collection in Europe. In the Spring the penguin parade starts again, where the cage door to their enclosure is opened at 2.15pm and the penguins voluntarily walk around their enclosure. That would not happen however till a few months yet so I decided I would try and talk to a parrot. First however, I had to find some!

The Parrot

One day, a few weeks later, Romany needed a new dog collar. So we went into a big pet store near Roslin, in Midlothian. Immediately when I entered my ears tuned into the cheeping of budgies. I went over to the cages and there was one with cockatiels and one with parrots. Immediately I knew these birds were not happy. It was the middle of the day and all but one of the parrots were sleeping and their coats were dull. I caught the eye of the one that was awake and asked the Fairy of this parrot what was wrong with them. It said *"The lights are too bright, and it is too cold for us."* I felt really sad. I wanted to take them all home but knew it was not practical.

I told the Fairy I was writing a book on Elementals and that St. Francis had said the parrots were special. She said, *"Yes, parrots are climate change indicators. Parrots can only live in the wild in certain temperature ranges."* How interesting I thought. *"Parrots bred in captivity struggle when the temperature is not right, that is why these look so ill."* I felt really sad when I left the shop and prayed for them to get help. I didn't even look for a dog collar after my chat with the Fairy. I sent the parrot healing thoughts. When I next returned to the shop, the parrots were gone. The store was to no longer stock them, when I enquired what had happened to them I was told they had all gone back to the breeder.

Return Of St Francis

St. Francis reappeared three weeks later after his first visit again to talk to me about birds. It was a beautiful sunny spring day and I was outside in the garden with Romany. This time he said, *"Birds I have told you about generally, now its time for me to get into specifics. Different birds have different roles. The parakeet is a climate indicator. It can spot changes in climate well in advance and move to hotter or colder areas. They can fly thousands of miles contrary to common belief. However, now their habitat is being* destroyed and many species are in grave danger. The penguin is another special bird. I wish you to visit them then they can tell you their story. The owls as you know are incarnate wise souls. The owls watch over Earth and inform Gaia/Geb what it is like to be living in the current time." What I had been told previously by the Fairies about owls is that they are souls of very special people who choose not to reincarnate again fully into human form because it is quite a painful process entering such a dense body. These souls called upon as owls will help any human who will acknowledge their being and power. It is important you try to communicate with the owls for healing the natural environment. The owls will try to attract human attention by giving you sightings to reawaken the part of you that knows the healing power of an owl, the Fairies explained to me. Leave out food for them in your garden and they will call. Admire their beauty and grace and allow them to communicate with you was what I was told.

Saint Francis continued, "I will now tell you about the common birds. The blackbird for example is the bird of the spirit. It connects people to the spirit world. The blackbird can awaken the spirituality within a person. Part of the reason blackbirds are common is because of this reason. They have many broods each year to reproduce as many young as possible. The blackbird is a respected bird in the bird community. It is probably the easiest bird for people to try to start bird communications with as it will speak back." I wondered if this was why I saw so many blackbirds when I was ill. I remember there was a particular male that used to sit on the roof of my neighbour's house every evening, just before the sun disappeared for the night. It would sit on the end ridge tile and sing every night. Perhaps the blackbirds were part of my spiritual awakening I now thought, as I had derived much comfort watching that particular bird. I was sure it knew I was there but I can't quite describe how.

Before suffering from this illness I did not believe in life after death or reincarnation. I did however believe there was a God and I had always had a firm belief in the Gaia hypothesis, which presents Mother Earth as a living breathing organism with the systems and cycles within all working hand in hand. The more I learnt from the Elementals the firmer my belief was in this theory. What was also interesting was that our ancestors have believed in much of what I was currently being told. Were they too in communication with these nature spirits I wondered?

Saint Francis continued his message to me, *"The blue tit on the other hand is a timid bird and it is a bird of peace. It is unfortunate that the white dove has been chosen as the symbol of peace when in fact it is the tit, in particular the blue tit. It is the vibration and energy of this species that make it special. Notice it does not fight unlike the robin or the sparrow; it is more tolerant of its neighbours. It symbolises harmony within the collective. It is a bird that leads by example."*

What St. Francis was saying rang true to me. I have rarely seen a blue tit fight. He now turned my attention to a bird that has prominent mythical beliefs: the crow. *"The crow is the bird of death. In ancient times it was considered bad luck however a crow will be attracted to a dying person but not for bad reasons. The crow energy prepares people for passing over, that is its purpose. The crow is not to be feared or scared of. It does a worthy job. The rook however is slightly different to the carrion. A rook is not as common as a crow their energy is different. The rook has no spiritual role from that point of view and should not be confused with the crow.*

The other birds that have specific spiritual roles are the hawk. The hawk is a bird of precision. The energy of the hawk, which one can draw on if they commune with hawks, is the energy of directness. If you wish to refrain from going round the bushes to straight to the heart of the matter the hawk can assist you. The falcon although also a bird of prey, is different again. It is the bird of prosperity. A picture of a falcon in one's house can bring in good luck and wind falls. There are many other birds that have healing energy also. The budgerigar is a healing bird as are many of the brightly coloured birds and the pelican. The healing birds produce healing frequencies for the earth and its inhabitants through their plumage and their call.

This is why it is therapeutic for a human to listen to their sound on CDs," he explained.

I found this particularly interesting because in the last few weeks the spring flowers had started to burst open, showering the countryside with brilliant yellows, purples and blues. I have recently become interested in the significance of colour for healing the environment. I think they must be vibrant for a reason so I made a mental note to speak to the Fairies about this at a later date.

The Swan

Saint Francis had given me detailed information on birds but soon I wanted to speak to a bird again. One day Richard and I stopped in Doune, near Stirling and visited the nature reserve. The energy was very low but as we walked further along the path through the trees we came to a big pond which had ducks and a couple of mute swans in it. One of the swans came towards the edge of the pool and sat looking at us. I had been told water birds have Sprites as guardians so I quieted my mind and tried to commune with the swan's Sprite. I asked the Sprite what it did for this swan.

The Sprite said to me, "*We are the swans' protector. Our job is to ensure its wings stay waterproof and no harm can come to it. The swan as a bird is the symbol of grace. It is here on Earth to remind people to be graceful on all occasions. The swan carries the frequencies of new growth with maturity. Swan energy also carries important frequencies for the fresh water it resides on for the plants and other creatures that live beneath. Swans unlike ducks require nourishment of the energetic kind. This means it cannot survive in polluted areas. You will rarely see a swan unless it is sick residing in mucky water. They fly to areas where the frequency is right for them. This is why you often find hundreds of swans residing in a particular loch and others with only one because of the frequencies a swan requires; they can only live in large groups where the high vibration energy is abundantly available. To see a swan on a water body indicates the presences of the special frequency of Chi* (life force) *that is sometimes referred to as "Kai Chi Chi" in Chinese literature. Kai Chi Chi means the Chi of the calibrated energies of the air, land and sea."*

How interesting, I knew of Chi from Feng Shui but had not delved too deeply into that topic. *"The countries that do not have swans in their water bodies do not carry the right vibrational frequencies of the Chi. If your wish is to bring this into your garden or home it is a good to place a statue of a swan in the vicinity you require this special Chi. The shape of the swan is unique,"* the Sprite explained.

Once the Sprite finished its message the swan started to swim round to join its mate further along the pond edge. It was interesting that six months previous to meeting this swan's Sprite, I had purchased a beautiful pink glass swan which now sits on my angel alter. I had felt compelled to buy it in the shop in Bridge of Allan and at the time did not know why the pull had been so great. Since the Sprites last words to me were, *"Remember swans are the birds of grace."* I decided to investigate ancient mythology regarding the swan. Richard has a set of Druid Animal Oracle cards and the card containing the swan claimed it represented the soul, grace and the beauty of the feminine. So the folklore and mythology connotations matched the Sprite's description.

The Bird Song

When I finally made it to Edinburgh Zoo it was Spring time and the penguin parade had begun again. As I stood waiting along with the tourists and parents with toddlers for the penguin gates to open, I noticed the penguins were very sociable birds gathering in huddles as if preparing for their walk. The penguins don't walk very fast but one penguin in particular caught my eye and I mentally asked that penguin's guardian to talk to me. The penguin had a guardian Sprite and its Sprite told me, *"Penguins are unusual birds because they cannot fly. The penguin only lives in the Southern Hemisphere you will not find them in the north. The spiritual role of the penguin is to be an energy anchor in regions that are too remote for human habitation. Penguins are very intelligent birds and they mate for life. Young penguins are looked after by their father until they are old enough to be out in the cold alone. Penguins you see are very in tune with the energy frequency changes on planet Earth and part of their job is to input the new required frequencies into the continent of Antarctica where they naturally live. Most creatures reside on Earth for a reason, they have a Divine purpose. The penguin is here to help balance the poles."*

I only had a short chat with the Sprite of the penguin because they kept walking as I tried to follow. However I thought this was an interesting concept that animals had a Divine life purpose too and that certain animals and birds perform particular roles for Planet Earth. I knew for example that dolphins had special roles too and this was well written about in Atlantean and Lemurian books. I wondered, after my visit to the zoo, what the part about frequencies really meant.

The next day I had an early morning visit from St. Francis. I was not even out of bed when I could feel his energy round about me in the room. He announced, *"Good morning! I have come to speak about the relationship between birds and trees. The trees play a vital role in bird ecology you see. Without trees the birds would loose habitat and food. The relationship between myself and the bird guardians are entwined. My role as an Ascended Master is to oversee and protect the animal kingdom in particular the bird kingdom. To do this I regularly commune with each species' guardian and the Tree Spirits. My job is to activate the soul within the tree once it has reached maturity, thereby coming of age in terms of its development on the wisdom and knowledge of the Earth in the past. Not every tree is activated by me. Only certain trees receive this process, they are specially located, usually on ley lines or earth energy centres. The tree then has a specific role to play as an energy cleaner of that area, which is why some trees feel more powerful than others.*

The relationship between the birds and the trees is a complex one. Bird song is so beautiful and distinct for a reason. The vibrational tones of the bird's song provide frequencies which activate the trees into bursting into bud. People think this process is climatic which it is to a certain extent, however, the vibrations of the bird song means the tree buds open sooner and the trees produce more leaves and fruit. In countries where the birds have been shot for sport and food the whole ecosystem of that area does not function accordingly or to its full supposed mechanism. Therefore imbalances are created. Man has interfered again in this respect too much. The song birds are of vital importance in the Spring to awaken the ecology of the countryside. The importance of bird song vibration cannot be overstated for the whole planet. This is why it is of vital importance we get the biodiversity balance back into the correct order."

I had not ever considered that there was any correlation between bird song and trees. The planet is even more linked that I had comprehended. Yet St. Francis was not finished with his messages for me and he continued, "I also want to talk to you about the importance of birds for the farmland. Again, farmland birds have an important role in germination of crops with the vibrational frequencies of their chirping. The birds' role is to awaken all other processes that relate to growth and development. That is why it is important for farmlands to have hedgerows for birds to nest in.

Also important is the moorhen and grouse on the hills this is because of their link with the heather. Heather is a very special plant often not regarded as such. Yet the old gypsy tale of white heather bringing good luck stems from their knowledge of the magical properties of different heathers. Unlike trees, heather has different frequencies that it emits out into the world. For example white heather is actually a protector. It is good to have planted at your front door. The luck that is associated with it is due to the belief that nothing bad can happen around your home. Purple heather on the other hand is a benefactor which brings your property luck. It is good not to have purple heather immediately outside your door but in your garden and in your house. I hope you are starting to see the interconnected roles that are played out by the whole of ecology. One can not function without the other and this is a key environmental message for your book," St Francis said.

Appreciation & Invocation

Thank you to Saint Francis for all his help with this chapter. St Francis is the patron saint of animals and birds. He helps with animal communication and healing and working with birds and nature. He will help anyone that is passionate about animals and the environment. St Francis comes to your side as soon as you think of him and therefore you do not necessarily have to say an invocation to bring him and his guidance into your life. To invoke St Francis to help you he asked that you say:

"St Francis patron saint of animals and birds, I ask for your loving guidance to help me on my Divine path. I know my role involves helping animals and birds and ask you to assist me in doing so."

Original Artist Unconfirmed

© Richard Kenchington

Chapter 9
The Spirit Of The Trees

The Wood Nymph I had met when writing the woodland chapter had told me of Tree Spirits and St Francis had mentioned them too. One day when walking Romany by the river I decided to see for myself if they really existed. The weather was cold and no leaves were yet back on the deciduous trees. The first Tree Spirit I had the pleasure of talking to was the guardian of an Ash tree. This tree had its roots in the water and they formed a pool which Romany was enjoying investigating. I stood by the tree and asked out loud if the tree's Elemental guardian would speak to me. To my delight I heard a masculine booming voice reply. He explained to me he was this tree's Tree Spirit and I explained to him I was writing a book on the Elementals. He agreed to give me some guidance. *"Trees are not just there to provide oxygen for the earth. We are wise and have seen many changes. I, myself am 152 years old. I have seen the changes of the landscape and the different energies of the time. As trees we each have a different story to tell,"* he said.

I knew trees have long been associated with ancient wisdom and the Celts and Druids believed each tree had a different spiritual role. The Tree Spirit continued, *"I want you to know that each tree has a different healing property so if you have a particular complaint or emotional issue you need to choose the specific tree for that purpose. Ash is the tree of wisdom. If you are looking for an answer to a why or a how, go to an Ash."* I liked this idea of sitting under specific trees to get answers to my problems, of which there were many at this time in my life! My old life of being a respected political researcher and policy officer was a far cry from being a spiritual writer, setting up my own business and people accepting that I could hear and see beings that were in another realm. I had to prove myself in a new field, one where there was much scepticism. I had to deal with people asking me for channelled personal information as to their Angel's advice and when they got an answer they did not like, reacting negatively against me.

All I am is the messenger, but I was finding it hard, particularly when they were friends. I had embraced this gift I had been given by God and was enjoying it very much but I cannot say it has been easy and I have had to make many difficult choices to be on my Divine path. Some of the choices I now know were tests to see if I would take the easy route out, others were in order to pursue my own happiness which I came to understand when I lay in my bed all that time, is the only thing that really matters in life. If you are unhappy in life, then only you can change that. I am now a firm believer that we create our own reality. It is always our own choice as to the thoughts that we think no matter how bad a situation is. When I was in my bed I had to take pleasure out of the little things in life like a bird hopping along the wall outside my bedroom window or a bush bursting into flower in my neighbour's garden. That time was, as well as being the worst time of my life, also an invaluable learning experience. I was forced to look inwards and at the way I thought about things.

As I have said before negative thoughts always made me feel worse, the pain was greater and the feelings that accompanied the tears were not pleasant. What was the point in being that way? I was just creating more misery for myself. When I felt grateful that on a particular morning I managed to be able to listen to a radio show or a chapter of an audio book and felt like I had achieved something positive, it always helped me inch just that bit further down the tunnel to my desired end result: complete recovery and being back to leading a full and happy life again. I certainly did find that being under a tree made me think about things that would not usually enter my head. I was by now so amazed by this glorious planet and all that went on unseen by humans except by a lucky enlightened few and I was truly excited about being able to allow more people through my writing to have the opportunity of having such experiences for themselves. I was especially excited about helping people to broaden their understanding of the systems of planet Earth. The Ash Tree Spirit finished our chat by saying that next, I should visit was a Beech tree.

Spring had finally arrived and I walked to the beech tree beside the cottage. It is a big tree formed now into the classic beech tree shape. I sat down underneath it, my back against its trunk. I mentally tuned into the Elemental realm. I was aware of the Wood Nymphs on the tree and the Fairies fluttering about around me in the grass. I asked the Beech tree's Elemental guardian to speak to me. Its Tree Spirit told me, *"Beech is the tree of justice. If you are trying to find the truth in situation then sit under a Beech tree and speak to its Tree Spirit about your problem."* The tree had not divulged exactly how it would help me find the truth in a situation but then again I had not asked. Elementals are a bit like humans in that some will tell you everything without you having to ask, but with others you need to ask more directly. Later that day I walked into the forest beside the cottage. On the outskirts of it is my favourite tree; the Pine with the bent trunk I mentioned in the woodland chapter. I found its Tree Spirit to be very friendly. He said to me, *"I am younger than those you have spoken to so far. I am the tree of freedom. If you are trying to break free of a situation or if you feel trapped by something or someone, sit under me. Discuss it and talk to me. Pine can make you see you have options and are always free."* Again the rain came on so I had to leave the conversation but I was definitely starting to think there was something different I could feel under each tree.

Tree Auras

Although now I had spoken to three Tree Spirits I did not know much about what they, as Elementals, actually did. This all changed when I spoke to a Scots Pine tree by the River Tweed. It was a sunny spring day and I had been speaking to the Water Sprites in the Tweed. Having stood for a while on the river bed, I looked about for somewhere to sit and rest. I still was unable to stand for long. The Scots Pine had low branches near the ground which looked like I could sit on. So I sat down and let the sun hit my face. As I relaxed in the sunlight, my body craving Vitamin D after so much house confinement over the previous years, the thought flashed through my mind; I haven't spoken to a Scots Pine Tree Spirit.

After a few minutes of letting the sunshine filter into the pale skin I had exposed I told the Pine Tree Spirit that I was writing a book and wanted to do a chapter on Tree Spirits. I heard a very deep, powerful, male voice speak back to me. "*A Tree Spirit is one of the oldest and wisest Elementals. We reside within the tree from the beginning, a bit like a soul resides within a human body. One cannot be without the other. Tree Spirits missions are to protect and safeguard the tree to our best abilities. We provide the energy for the natural biological systems to take place; like the soul within a human provides the life-force. The Tree Spirit also has the job of protecting all creatures dwelling in or on their tree. We invite the Wood Nymphs to join our branches, to tend to our leaves and bark and to stop invasion of any disease if possible. Like humans, trees have auras. Chemicals destroy our auras, just like they do a human's. When we are sprayed for protecting our fruit, if a fruit tree, we become more susceptible to disease and parasites. Chemical sprays from fields such as herbicides and pesticides do the same as does acid rain and air pollution. This is why trees respond well to healing vibrations sent to them. Tree Spirits are powerful healers. We are the most powerful Elemental healer for a landscape and a human,*" the Tree Spirit said.

Some trees are very vibrant, yet others feel dull. I had noted that the ones whose energy felt subdued were often along arable fields. It had never occurred to me however that they too are affected by pesticides, herbicides and insecticides that are sprayed on the fields. But then why would they not be? For example, you would not eat rat poison because the poison may kill you too and if not would most certainly make you very ill. So why do we humans think that a chemical that is used to kill an insect or a weed (which is just a plant growing in the wrong place) would not harm a tree growing beside it? The roots soak up the soil water which the chemical has filtered into, and the leaves are hit by the spray blown off course by the wind.

All of a sudden I felt a great jolt inside me with this realization. Rachel Carson in her, now iconic, book 'Silent Spring' had warned us 50 years ago that our actions are affecting all systems not just the one it is intended for, because the environment is all intrinsically linked. I stared out across the valley, the hill tops visible above the forestry line and Dawyck Botanical Gardens with its vast collection of magnificent trees from all over the world, straight ahead. The Tree Spirit had said that trees have auras. I had only recently started to understand about the human aura so it had never occurred to me that other living creatures might have them too. The aura is the energy field around a person that is mostly invisible. The only time most humans really get the sense of their auras is in one of two situations I think and even then we don't necessarily appreciate what we are sensing. How many of you have gone on a busy bus or train and the person you are sat beside feels too close for comfort yet you are not touching at all?

Well they are within your auric field and as you don't know them or are incompatible with their energy frequency it feels uncomfortable. The other extreme is when you are lying in your partner's arms and that can feel like the nicest thing in the world. Your auras are merging at that point on the energetic level as well as being physically close. Some people have the ability to see auras. These people can see colour around people and can tell from the colour what may be an issue for that particular person. They can also scan the aura for areas of weakness. Often an area of auric weakness coincides with an area of physical ill health. Since human auras can be interfered with by various things it is no real surprise that tree auras are affected by chemicals and pollution. Yet finding out trees had auras was very exciting. The Tree Spirit continued to tell me that a fruit tree that has a healthy aura produces lots of fruit. I have since been able to see healthy tree auras and they show as a blue haze around a tree. It is a very beautiful sight when the tree is happy and in good health. They seem to radiate their joy out across the land.

The Scots Pine Tree Spirit then started talking to me about Tree Spirits' roles on the planet, *"The Tree Spirit also is an energy anchor, but what we do is give that energy to the Air Spirit like the Gnomes do for the land. The trees not only output vital oxygen so that Mother Earth can breathe but we provide the purified energy for the Sylphs, Sylphons and Spirulites,"* he said. Spirulites were new Elementals to me! I had never heard of them. The Tree Spirit explained to me that Spirulites are the Air Spirits who look after the rain and snow as it falls. *"The Spirulites cover the land when there is snow. Each element or force has a guardian,"* he said. I hadn't actually thought about snow as needing a guardian but then in some parts of the world the ground is always covered in snow. My mind was starting to wonder thinking about the possible Spirulite roles and activities when the Tree Spirit brought my attention back to him. *"As a Scots Pine my particular area of expertise is weathering the storm. My tree frequency sees people through the rough times and shows them the end is near. I can provide support and channel the frequencies the human body needs through a difficult time. I am best visited when in the midst of a crisis to show you when it will end and how to get through it to a new beginning,"* I was told. As I walked away from the majestic Scots Pine after thanking it for its help my brain still did not understand how they put frequencies into humans and animals. I did not get a greater understanding of the Tree Spirit's frequency role until I spoke to the Tree Spirit of a Lime tree, again along the banks of the River Tweed on another dog walk.

It was a summer's evening, although not very warm. I hadn't yet spoken to a Lime tree so I sat under the branches of this tree and I tuned into its Tree Spirit. It talked to me immediately. He said I needed more information on tree auras which I wholeheartedly agreed with. All the Tree Spirits I have communed with have had a male voice, in case you wondered.

The Tree Spirit said to me, "*Tree auras are very important to trees. It is part of a Tree Spirit's job to ensure the aura stays as healthy as possible. The aura of a tree can show the state a tree is in emotionally. We are badly affected by disease and climatic changes naturally, but in the last hundred years or so, pollution has become our big issue.*" Like all the Elementals I have met they have mentioned pollution as hindering and affecting them.

The Tree Spirit continued, "*Trees get nutrients from the ground but our interaction with the air is of great importance. The aura of a tree is how we communicate with the Sylphons and Sylphs to energetically exchange. You are currently sitting under my tree therefore you are within this tree's auric field. The auric field of each tree is different depending on the tree type. Also depending on the state of your auric field as a human you will receive certain benefits from sitting under a certain type of tree. My tree's healing power is that of emotional relaxation. If one has been under emotional stress they should visit a Lime. In a way we work like crystals do. Our auric frequency can input frequencies into your auric field when they are required which can heal.*" Ah ha, an exchange I thought, or possibly just a hole being filled. He continued, "*Trees often get sick and require healing through receiving the energetic frequencies themselves. It would be good to train people to give tree healings. Teach them to act as channels for the certain frequencies that trees require. You will feel the difference in the tree in question almost immediately. Prior to human destruction of the natural systems of the environment we did not require this to be done but due to genetic engineering of trees, chemical sprays and acid rain we find ourselves often energetically depleted.*"

I was very conscious by now that I was actually physically relaxing under this tree. My shoulders had relaxed greatly and I felt like I was bathing in its energy and my body was getting something it needed. The Tree Spirit explained to me, "*Humans are no different to any other living creature. A plant, an animal, a bird can all suffer emotional stress. Trees developed to put out these healing frequencies into the environment, so we can all work in harmony.*" This statement took my mind back to what I learned when I studied Environmental Archaeology. After the last ice age in Scotland circa 10,000 years ago, trees re-colonised the land in a sequence. First was Birch and Ash and later came Oak, Beech and Sycamore. Was the colonisation purely an environmental factor or were there energetic factors also? Much of regular science is still just theory and speculation. Perhaps, at that time, the Earth needed the energetic frequencies that those particular trees carried in that order.

Next I decided to search out an Oak tree. This Oak Tree Spirit I found in Perthshire surrounded by arable fields and looming above my Dad's bee hives. The Tree Spirit said to me, "*I have been with this Oak tree for one hundred and thirty years. The Oak is the tree of patience. The frequency we give out helps people to see that sometimes one has to wait for no explainable reason for what they want. Patience is a virtue few humans truly possess. The energy of the Oak can help grant it. The Oak trees have other special roles on the planet too. We are the trees of purification for the ground. Our roots help more than any other native tree in Scotland to soak up nitrogen. We also help to fertilise the ground through our roots unlike any other tree. We do this by storing nutrients and giving them when the ground needs it. The soil plays an important part in the ecosystems of the earth; unfortunately modern farming methods however have interfered with this process. There was a reason trees were planted around the fields. Ancient civilisations knew about our role in protecting soil and working with it in exchanging nutrients. Trees you see are anchors. We interact with all the ecosystems in some way. It is our job as Tree Spirits to be aware that we harness energy and direct it through using our knowledge and wisdom. We are in residence in a tree for so many years that we witness the change in the landscape and human behaviour.*" So naturally I asked what he had witnessed. "*I have seen so many changes. These fields were ploughed by horse and cart, now by big machines. Poly tunnels have sprouted up over the last few years creating artificial conditions for plants. They now grow at the wrong time, taking nutrients from already depleted soils. Natural seasons are now lost,*" he said sadly. I asked him what do the Tree Spirits want done. "*Remove nasty chemicals from your farming* methods and return to restoring natural balance to the soils. *Nature has all the answers.*" I stood up from the stone I was sitting on under his mighty Oak. I thanked the Tree Spirit for imparting its knowledge. I was by now getting the message loud and clear from the trees. They don't like chemicals!

Dawyck Botanical Gardens

My next meeting with a Tree Spirit was a couple of months later. It was the start of Autumn. I wanted to visit Dawyck Botanical Gardens, in Stobo, the Scottish Borders because I had looked out over these trees every day from the cottage. So one Saturday afternoon we took a trip there. I was still unable to walk very far uphill, so stuck to the low level trees (the gardens are on the side of a relatively steep hill). Most of the trees in the gardens are foreign. I stopped at a tree whose family is called Cupressaceae. Its label said it was an American species. I sat beneath it and mentally asked its Tree Spirit if it would commune with me. The Tree Spirit told me, "*My tree is the American Tree of Courage. If one needs to be courageous one should stand within the aura of my tree type. Bravery will come from within. I can put the frequencies required that are missing in your energy field in so that you will have the courage to tackle any situation you need help with.*"

   This led me to ask a question my friend Leila wanted to know about trees. Was it the tree itself or the Tree Spirit that did this? "*It is the Tree Spirit who controls the output frequency of the tree. So if the tree is sick so are its Tree Spirit and Wood Nymphs. Pollution you see allows disease to enter as trees, like humans, have immune systems. If humans eat unhealthy foods which contain no minerals or have toxic ingredients then your immune system struggles. You get colds and flu or even worse conditions; the same happens to trees. Some trees are more susceptible than others to this type of energetic imbalance. It is the same with some humans depending on the genetic makeup of the individual. With the trees it tends to be species where the genetic makeup of that species means they struggle even more. For example this is the case with Elms, hence Dutch Elm disease.*"

I was really excited that this Tree Spirit was talking to me about Dutch Elm disease. I studied Elms at University and I had recently seen a whole row of Elms who were dead or affected with this disease which had upset me. The Tree Spirit went on to explain, *"Contrary to general belief it is environmental factors that have caused this terrible disease that have wiped Elms out. It is the Tree Spirit's job to ensure a tree doesn't get sick however the Tree Spirits of Elms are under greater stress as their tree really struggles with airborne pollution. It requires a lot of energetic power from the Tree Spirit within to counteract the effects of the daily living conditions of the trees. It has however gone far out of the tolerance levels for Elms so this disease has come in."* I fully understood what this Tree Spirit was saying. Environmental stress causing physical stress resulting in disease or ill health is a well known biological process. Just as some humans are more susceptible to environmental (as in their environment) problems, tree types are too. Meeting and listening to the Elementals, hearing the problems our current human lifestyles are causing the natural world really was hitting home. Although I had studied all this from a scientific and political point of view it never hit me as much as it did at this precise moment. I felt like there must be more I could do.

Walking further along the path all these beautiful and majestic trees were singing their own tunes in the breeze that was now picking up. I then came across a tree I had been keen to talk to, a Yew. There were four of them together. I stood under one and asked its Tree Spirit what healing frequencies the Yew offered. Its Tree Spirit spoke to me, *"The Yew is the tree of fortitude. It is often regarded as a sacred tree. We are situated at graveyards near churches as we are thought to be protectors. The Yew is in fact a symbol of chastity and purity, so what we do in graveyards is cleanse the souls that come to grieve."* I was a bit confused about this message. What did chastity have to do with fortitude? The Tree Spirit of the Yew explained, *"We fortify the mourners, giving them strength to carry on by removing what is stopping them. It is not that* we ward off evil, it is that we stop evil being attracted to those distraught souls." The thought of evil made me shudder. The path   I was on led to the chapel in the grounds. Yews are not my favourite type of tree but I thanked the Tree Spirit for its message and I walked a bit further looking for another species. The sky above had turned grey and it was starting to rain. The temperature was dropping as it was now late afternoon. We decided to head home, the dog was in the car and no doubt getting bored and I was getting hungry. As we walked along the path to the exit a tree caught my eye. It was an Acer and when I got closer I could feel its very bubbly nature. I knew it had a message and I think its message is a good one to end the tree chapter on because it reminded me that even in time of great distress, anguish and concern we need to remember that fun and laughter are great healers. The Acer Tree Spirit put a smile on my face with this message, *"The Acer is the tree of mystery. If you need any puzzle solving come sit under me. If your brain feels blocked and you cannot see to solve the clue, then that is what I am here to do. Come tell me your puzzle, I will help all I can. I am the tree of mystery that is what I am."*

Appreciation & Invocation

Thank you to Rhiannon for helping with this chapter. Rhiannon gave this message for you:

"I am a Welsh Celtic Goddess of the enchanted woodland. My job is to watch over the woodland, the bird kingdom, the animals and plants too. I can facilitate remembrance of why you as a soul are here and the job you need to do. Trees are of vital importance to the whole ecosystem. I encourage you all to commune with trees, receive their healings and wisdom. To invoke me all you need to say is: Beautiful Rhiannon come to my side now. Help guide me to the trees that can help me most with my Divine mission and heal me too. Help to tune into the tree frequencies and to carry these frequencies with me in my daily life. Thank you Rhiannon for all the blessing you now bestow on me."

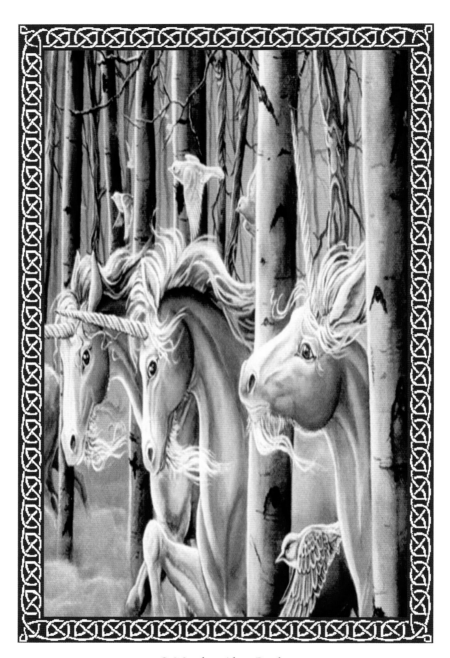

© Marilyn Alice Boyle

Chapter 10
The Unicorns

Often portrayed as a beautiful white horse with a long mane and a shimmering horn protruding from its head, the Unicorn is considered the ultimate magical creature. I vividly remember the day the idea that Unicorns existed was dropped into my head. Whilst walking past a birch wood I said to Richard, and the dog, *"Unicorns live in that forest!"* I even surprised myself when the words flowed out of my mouth. It was as if they had been put there by someone else. Perhaps it was the Unicorns calling me, however from that moment I knew Unicorns were real and not just creatures created for children's tales.

Slightly in shock from my statement, and at the same time touched by the beauty of the energy I could feel around the birch wood, I was engulfed in waves of tingles all through my body. I knew by this point in my spiritual path that this is a sign that I have understood something correctly. Usually however, when I have acknowledged the existence of an Elemental group I am really keen to communicate with them. This was not the case with the Unicorns. Although their energy was wonderful and seemed to engulf every pore in my body when I tuned into it, I felt in no hurry to speak to them. Something told me I would be back here and would speak to them when the time was right.

It was not long after first becoming aware of the Unicorns that I had my first experience of meeting them. What I found out is that the Unicorns must invite you to meet them. Richard and I were invited into the birch wood one afternoon and we sat quietly on an old tree stump amongst the ferns. Three Unicorns appeared at the edge of the wood clearing. They were smaller than I expected; the size of a Shetland pony but the physique of a horse. They had a spiralling golden horn protruding from their head between their ears. I could see and feel they were timid creatures. As they stood looking at us still metres away, I sensed that they were not coming closer because the masculine part of Richard's energy was too harsh for them. These were creatures of such beauty and gentleness it was an amazing feeling to be in their presence. Richard softened his energy, a process we can all do through deep breathing and letting go of negativity, replacing it with a feeling of peace and emanating pure love, and they came closer and circled us.

Their energy was loving and healing. As they were circling us I asked if they had lived at this location for long. One of the Unicorns telepathically said to me, *"We have lived here for thousands of years."* They liked it here because few people entered this exclusive, remote birch wood. I asked how many of them here there were. The reply was one hundred and eighteen of them. I had not thought that there would be so many. They slowly circled us three times and then disappeared back into the wood. Before they had started to circle us I had been told it would be a short experience the first time we received a Unicorn healing, but that we were welcome to visit again. As we walked out of the wood, I felt a mixture of exhilaration and excitement. My first Unicorn experience and they had invited us to meet them again.

Healing The Heart

My second experience with the Unicorns lasted longer and had a much more profound affect on me. We were again taking Romany for a walk and as we walked past the birch wood I was aware of the Unicorns' energy. I ignored it as we had the dog with us and I had been told that the Unicorns were not keen on his boisterous energy. We walked further up the track and stopped to listen and watch a flock of long tailed tits. I found that I was tired, I was still building up my walking and stamina and the track was uphill, so we called Romany but he was nowhere to be seen. Richard said to just head back and he would find us. As we walked down the track I told Richard I was being called into the clearing in the birch wood. We found a large white quartz stone and sat down. As we sat I then saw a large male Unicorn come towards us. He was bigger than the ones we met previously. He told me that Romany had been called away so we could have a Unicorn healing. He then stood in front of us and told us to touch his golden horn.

I did so where I thought his horn was but I felt nothing. He then started to circle us and a female Unicorn appeared. I assumed she was female as she was smaller. They circled us in a figure of eight. All of a sudden I felt love being poured into my heart and my heart becoming lighter. I could see things being pulled from both our hearts. I am not exactly sure what as they were, just a blur of shapes. Then two more Unicorns appeared! We were now being circled in a figure of eight by four Unicorns. The large male Unicorn started to speak. He said we had been given the gift of Unicorn healing and could now call on them when we needed love and protection. *"Only the purest of heart can be given this gift. We have severed the ties and cords to previous relationships and situations that have caused your hearts pain,"* he explained. I then saw the Unicorns walk back towards the trees.

However, the female Unicorn was lingering. I heard the male Unicorn say, *"Come our job is done,"* but she stood still then walked towards Richard. She started to circle him and she said they had not lifted all the pain from his heart. I sat quietly for a short time until they were done. Richard said he could not see anything that was happening but could feel it. The Unicorns left this time and headed back deep into the woods. I had originally wanted to go back to the house because I had felt tired. Now I felt full of energy, elated and lighter. It is hard to describe in words the experience of receiving healing from Unicorns, except to say it is an overwhelming experience of love, the purest kind of love which just radiates from these magnificent creatures right into the core essence of one's being; an experience of pure love from one soul to another soul; a reminder that to love truly is all that is important to the world. As we walked back to the track still bathing in the Unicorn energy, the dog was still not in sight. Unconcerned, based on the Unicorn's message, I called on Archangel Chamuel and my Guardian Angel to guide him back. Sure enough Romany soon came bounding down the track.

Golden Threads

My next Unicorn experience was by myself. I had been walking Romany one afternoon when I heard them calling me so I moved into their part of the wood. The dog was off running in the pine forest so I stood at the clearing near the birch wood. I could feel their magical energy about me. Then four beautiful white Unicorns trotted out of the wood and surrounded me. The feeling I experienced was of warmth and love. I felt like I was in a ball of love being infused with divine light. I started to feel very 'clean' as if stuff was being removed from my heart and as it was leaving, my heart felt lighter. Like a black ball had been lifted out. A ball I did not even know was in there. As I was experiencing this sensation one of the Unicorns spoke. She said, *"You all carry a weight in your heart. Only those who have never been hurt carry no weight. We have removed debris of hurt and pain from your previous relationships which you no longer need to carry in your heart chakra."* I thanked the Unicorns for their love and help and sent them blessings of love. They disappeared into the wood.

The Unicorns were so gentle and pure because the whole essence of their being and existence was to radiate love. I felt very blessed to have experienced not just once but by now three times a healing session from them. Each time after I felt a noticeable difference in my heart chakra and as a person I felt purer. It did feel like old pains and heartaches had been dissolved away. I was also conscious that the more I worked on cleaning my heart chakra, bringing in to my heart Divine love and releasing all negativity and fear on a regular basis, the easier it had become to commune with the Elementals. I had been

106

working with Angels to receive healing for a while now but being out in nature receiving healing from Elementals I found to be such a profound joy. The Unicorns were evidently excellent transmuters of pain and I felt so grateful for their existence in the world.

The Head Unicorn

Although I had now experienced Unicorn healing on various occasions, they had largely been silent with the Unicorns only telling me what was necessary at those times. I was therefore delighted one day when the head Unicorn, as he called himself, appeared and began to talk to me. *"You have now had three or four Unicorn healing sessions led by me and some others. We were very pleased when you noticed our Unicorn energy in the birch forest. Part of our healing role is to help initiated ones awaken. Only advanced energy souls can see and commune with Unicorns. We are special sentient beings and probably out of all the Elementals are affected by human feelings the most. This is why we only live in the most remote woods where few humans dwell. Birch is our favourite type of tree. Its energy resonates well with us and its healing powers are similar."*

I remembered how the Unicorn had said they had lived here for thousands of years. At university I had completed an environmental archaeology course as part of my environmental degree. That course looked at the Holocene period, which in Scotland is the period from the end of the last ice age circa 10,000 years ago until the present time. We studied the colonisation of trees after the ice's retreat and birch was one of the first colonisers of Scotland after the ice melted. The whole county would have been covered in swathes of birch wood. I smiled as I imagined Unicorns living everywhere in Scotland.

The head Unicorn drew my attention back to him saying, *"The Unicorn as an Elemental being's role is to protect the love that is within the planet. We are beings who emanate love and our job is to anchor the love into the earth and the rest of the Elemental Kingdom. We do this by* having pure hearts. Unlike the Fairies and Pixies we are not ever mischievous or playful. We are serious and sombre creatures but very beautiful too. Our horns are infused with golden divine power which stream out from our horn tip in golden beautiful rays. Our coats are white and our manes are curly and long. One time Unicorns graced the whole British Isles before all the deforestation took place. There are few birch woods these days that are left alone so we exist in a few locations in big numbers."

I had known that birch woods had a special energy, and I had assumed that was why the Unicorns' existed there but it was good to get confirmation from the Unicorns themselves. I therefore asked him if could tell me more about Unicorns. The reply came, "Yes, Unicorns' magical healing powers are unique. We are the ultimate healing Elemental for the human heart. The love that one feels when communing with a Unicorn is truly magnificent, as you have indeed felt I am sure. When a human places a hand on the coat of a Unicorn, love pours out. When communicating with Unicorns there is etiquette however. Before approaching an area where Unicorns are known to exist or where you feel Unicorn energy it is always good to ask if you can enter (mentally or aloud) or better still to wait to be asked to enter. More often than not you will find the Unicorns will invite you into their domain. We are however very timid creatures and communing with us requires patience and purity of heart. Much etheric work is required before meeting a Unicorn. They will not come to you until you are ready to meet them. Often the first meeting is not a healing session but a greeting to familiarise yourself with the Unicorns and their energy. True belief in our existence is of vital importance before any healing session will occur. We are creatures who have the gift of knowing the truth. No one can fool us as our sentience skills mean we can feel what is in the heart of a person and their beliefs."

He continued, "You have a guardian Unicorn. Her name is Friesha. She wishes to commune with you more and work with you to protect you from hurt and bring more divine love your way. She works with your other guardians and Elemental guides to help you fulfill your divine mission. Few people are assigned a guardian Unicorn but you have worked extensively with us in the past. You know many of our magic gifts and skills and now is the time to awaken them. The crystal rose quartz resonances well with us. Hence you love to carry this crystal." This is true. Rose quartz is my favourite crystal and I often wear it or carry a piece in my pocket. I sleep with a big piece beside my bed at night also.

He finished our chat by saying. "Feel this crystal's energy and feel our Unicorn energy. There is almost no difference. The rose quartz is the crystal of pure divine love. You should bring even more rose quartz into your life. It will facilitate more Unicorn communication and blessings and open you up more to the remembrance of our healing." I have always found it easier to communicate with Elementals and Angels if I am holding a crystal. I usually just use clear quartz as it is an amplifier but I have found there are certain specific crystals good for assisting talking to the different groups, like Rose Quartz for talking to the Unicorns, which I will explain further in a later chapter. I now regularly go to the birch wood to see the Unicorns and feel their special energy. The head Unicorn was also right in that they have helped awaken magical skills within me but most of all they have reminded me about the importance of love.

Appreciation & Invocation

I'd like to thank the Goddess Atheea, Goddess of the stars for helping me write this chapter. The head Unicorn told me that there was little written about her and indeed I found none in my search. However she came when I called her and helped this chapter reach fruition. To call on her for assistance say:

"Goddess Atheea, beauty of all that is light I ask you to help heal my blocks to communication with the unseen world of these Elementals. Help me to elevate through keeping myself etherically clean and elevate my intentions and desires to the purest form thus I may to have the blessing of meeting these unique creatures, the Unicorns, that you help watch over. Thank you Goddess Atheea, Goddess of the stars!"

© Jane Starr Weils

Chapter 11
Mermaids Are Real

So I had just found out that Unicorns are real and living in their dimension. Although I fully believed in their existence and had indeed seen, heard and felt them, the rational part of my brain still tried to argue with me at times. I still had the odd moment of, is this really happening to me? I didn't for a moment now doubt the Elementals' existence. I knew I believed in them or I wouldn't have had these experiences but still sometimes other people's doubt got to me. I wanted to get away from my familiar surroundings. I was being called to the sea. The Water Sprites had told me that Ocean Sprites existed in salt water and I thought a trip to the coast would be good. The Fife coast on the east coast of Scotland holds lots of childhood memories for me, mostly of summer holidays spent on St. Andrew's beach. So we set off to a place called Cellardyke in Fife. The B&B we checked into was right on the coast, perfect for Ocean Sprite hunting.

The Ocean Sprites live mostly in the surf or on the crest of waves, and like their equivalent in fresh water, Ocean Sprites are very joyful and playful Elementals. I chose a spot where there were lots of sea birds and ducks residing on the rocks and water as I knew from Saint Francis that sea birds have Sprites as their guardians. I sat on a large rock and centred my energy. By now I had communed with lots of different Elemental groups and my sixth sense had advanced a lot since I had started on my journey. I had found that like most things it becomes easier to communicate with nature spirits the more you practice it.

I became aware of movement in the rock pool in front of me although I could physically see nothing in the water left by the receding tide. Then I heard noise. This was clear and as if someone or some people were speaking right in front of me.

Again nothing was physically visible to me. The next thing I knew, I heard chanting! *"We Ocean Sprites are the guardians of the waves."* There were at least five voices. I looked again consciously trying to use my third eye this time.

The beach at Cellardyke is stony and big boulders are interspersed by flat slabs of rocks when the tide was this far out. The Isle of May, with its prominent lighthouse was just visible on the horizon with the sunshine creating a haze in the distance. *"We Ocean Sprites are similar to the Water Sprites you met at the river but we are slightly bigger in size. Our role is to energetically clean the sea water. There are billions of us worldwide doing this job,"* I was told. I remembered what the Water Sprites had said about using the natural physical power of the rapids to strengthen their energy systems to keep the rivers clean.

The Ocean Sprites who were talking to me continued, *"We use the wave energy in the same way the Water Sprites use the rapids' energy to give us power to do our job. Our magical powers are strengthened by a supply of energy from the elements, in our case the wind. We wish you to emphasis the importance of protecting the seas in your book. This is our home and it is being destroyed with human disregard and disrespect for the living world. Not only does raw sewage create disease but it affects the energetic frequency and lowers the vibrations of the sea's vital healing roles for all living things including us. The sea is of great importance to the earth, making the earth unique in your galaxy. The sea is what allows the earth to breathe."* There was an air of urgency in their voice. The message from them was clear. We as a race were having a colossal impact on the ecosystem of the sea on all levels.

I remembered back to studying oceanography at university. The seas and oceans have such an intricate structure. All it takes is one aspect to go out of balance and the whole system is affected. Man for many years has seen the sea as an expansive dumping ground, claiming the dilution theory as justification. The Sprites expanded on their concerns stating, *"Chemical pollution, oil spills and nuclear dumping are all affecting the natural* physical systems within the sea, and therefore they are having a great impact too on the energetic systems of the oceans and seas. Many Sprites are struggling to keep up their energetic cleaning role and are not able to do their job. Think what it is like when you are in a room full of smoke or fumes or dirt. It is much healthier and easier to work and live in a clean environment. The same is true for us. Please encourage people to think about their actions as an individual and as a race. At this time we need lightworkers help. We need help to stop the destruction of the seas, not only for us but for the Pixies, Undines, and Merpeople too." There was an air of desperation and also sadness in their voices. I told them, "I will help. I will get lightworkers' attention and get them to help. I will hold courses by the sea and conduct healing and meditations whatever you wish."

I felt a huge sigh of relief from the Ocean Sprites after I said this. Only one of them was talking and directly to me now, the rest were silent. I therefore asked this Sprite what they as an Elemental group looked like to help me better see them. He said, "We are usually always male in appearance although there are some tribes who take female form. We have beards and wear square topped hats. We also wear what you call shorts and no shoes." He then added, "We have another role. Not us but other Ocean Sprites are the guardians of sea birds. Their job is to watch over and protect sea gulls, guillemots, puffins, to name a few. It tends to be the female tribe who take on this role. Each bird has one guardian Sprite to look after its soul in its incarnation as a sea bird."

As the Sprite said this my eyes were drawn to a gull flying over the sea about twenty metres ahead of me. It made me smile to think of an invisible Sprite flying along with it. This begged the question of Sprites having wings. I was told, "No. We don't have wings, it is not necessary for us to have wings. It is not necessary for any Elemental to have wings because we can move freely within reason. Unlike an Angel we are constrained to a place depending on what our role is on earth. The Sprite just travels with the sea bird in its energy field." It was interesting the Sprites said no Elemental needs wings; some just choose to have them. As I was pondering this thought another one entered my head. The Sprites had mentioned Merpeople! I had never thought about Mermaids before except as mythical beings in children's tales. I asked the Sprites if there were any Mermaids in these waters. He said *"Of course there are Mermaids anywhere there are large mammals. The Mermaids protect the dolphins and the seals around these shores but Mermen live here too."*

This was another mind blowing revelation for me. Another much loved character of my childhood was real only they lived in a different dimension: the Elemental one. I firmly believe that as with all beings of the Devic Kingdom, true belief in their existence or an open mind at the possibility is all that is required to have contact with these special guardians of the natural world. My faith is always returned at moments like this as I know that I could not make any of this up. I was rarely imaginative, even as a child I always wrote factual essays in English class rather than fiction if I had the choice. My left brain worked over drive at university and when I worked in politics. I genuinely think my right brain only woke up when I was ill and decided to start to participate in my life. I was glad it had now, as I was enjoying not having to over analyse and make sense of everything. I just accepted that things could just be, and are.

Mermaid Appearance

I turned my gaze to look further along the beach. I had done this without knowing why. I could then see quite clearly three Mermaids' heads staring at me from the water. Their upper bodies then emerged as they watched me looking at them hardly believing my eyes. The image is still vivid in my memory: three smiling Mermaids, one of them waving. She had long ginger hair and a bright turquoise tale. It is unusual for me to see etheric beings in colour.

I moved closer to them. The one waving started to speak to me. *"We are the guardians of the oceans our role is to protect the large* sea dwelling mammals including humans in our seas. Currently the sea is in much turmoil. The climate change and rising temperatures are having a great impact on the whales, dolphins, sharks and coral to name a few species. We wish for less chemicals going into the water from boats, fish farms, pipes and getting out of balance to dangerous levels. Never before have we been so concerned."

I asked her what we could do to help. She replied, "You humans can start to change your ways. Look for new solutions, less pollution, new ways and technologies to live your lives. We particularly want lightworkers to work with us to access our healing power and rekindle the knowledge in your souls you all have."

I asked her which crystals help communication with Mermaids. She said, "Good crystals for Mermaids are Calcite, Aragonite and Malachite. They resonate well with us." I then asked her about life as a Mermaid. She told me, "We Merpeople live in what we call tribes but you might call it a family unit. We spend most of the time under water although we get extra power by basking on rocks in sun or moonlight. We have healing powers for animals, plants and humans. Ocean life is teaming with different organisms. We look after them all. You are getting cold, you should go in." And with that they dived under the ocean again leaving me slightly dazed that I had spoken to a Mermaid!

Merman Healing

The next day was very cold and windy when we took a trip to St Andrews, the beautiful ancient university town and, of course, the home of golf. We sat in the Landrover beside the sand dunes, the rain was drizzling down. I really didn't feel like venturing out of the car, however I was told by Sedna (the Goddess of the Sea and protector of all sea dwelling creatures), that I had to walk into the water and the Merpeople would heal me.

It would be a different healing to the one that the Unicorns gave me as it would be a more grounded healing. This surprised me as I never thought that standing in the ocean could be classified as a grounding experience, however if you think that the seas and oceans cover 80 percent of Earth's surface, standing in it is still an anchoring mechanism.

When I got down to the shore I was aware of lots of Sprites on the surface. I couldn't hear or see them but could feel their presences. As I knew I was tired and not really in the mood for this, I was not as open as I could have been to the whole experience. I was standing at the water's edge and Sedna said to me, *"You have to walk into the water. It is too shallow for them to come heal you here."* I walked until the water was over my ankles. I then thought I could see a Mermaid in my mind's eye on top of the breaking waves. She started waving at me. At the same time I could here a man's voice. He said, *"I am a Merman and I am anchoring you firmly to the sea-bed. This process will help bring down your higher self more easily."*

I then looked down and my 'welly' boots were being sucked down into the sand. I know this occurs when standing in a current but I could feel myself being pulled down into the sand I was standing on. It was an intriguing experience because I had for a month now been working on embodying my higher self with great difficulty in meditations. However I had not thought to ask Elementals for help with this task. I decided I would visit the coast more often and chat more with Mermaids. I wanted more healing from them which they freely give to those who are genuine and care about their environment and homes.

Guardian Mermaid

As I sat writing up my experiences in Fife for this chapter I started to hear someone speaking in my ear. Intrigued to see if I was to be introduced to another Elemental group that I knew nothing about, I asked who it was. To my surprise a female voice replied saying, *"I am your Guardian Mermaid."* Yes, I was told by her she is my Guardian Mermaid! I knew I had Guardian Angels and a Guardian Unicorn but a Mermaid too?!

116

I had to find out what these Guardian Elementals are and do for us! She told me her job was to protect me when I was in or around water. She said to me, "*Mermaids' and Mermens' healing gifts are to protect the habitat of sea dwelling creatures in the oceans and seas. We look after humans who travel on our seas and try to safeguard them from disaster in the treacherous waves. Legends always begin with a grain of truth. We exist in vast numbers all over the world yet we are probably the least believed Elementals of the oceans. Our lifestyle has had to change greatly since the advent of industrial fishing. The seas have become so much more polluted and it is affecting our homes and our numbers on earth are dwindling.*

Merpeople are very sensitive beings, and like the Unicorns we have been around for many thousands of years. We are not shy Elementals however and love to chat to humans and help them when they ask for our help. We Mermaids can grant wishes like Fairies but few people choose to manifest with us. That saddens us. We would especially like to help with any projects to reduce pollution, biodiversity loss and dumping in our seas.

We ask you to encourage people to come and talk to us when they are by the sea. It is easier for us to commune if you enter the water. Just standing in it is enough. Call out to us with your heart. You will find many of us will answer your call and appear to help ease your concerns and heal any pain. It is a joyous experience for us when a human believes we exist and call out for help. This is all part of our divine mission on earth. Please pass this message on to as many people as you can that we exist, we want to help and we want to work with you to protect our seas."

The Mermaids definitely were keen to get us to help the oceans but are also keen for us as a race to work with them and communicate with them to protect their animals and homes. The number of Elementals I had met so far had exceeded any expectations of the number of groups I would meet when I started this journey and I wondered who I would meet next.

Appreciation & Invocation

Thank you to the Goddess Sedna, Goddess of the Sea, for her help with this chapter. To invoke Sedna stand beside the sea or in view of the ocean and call out to her by saying:

"Sedna, powerful Goddess of the Sea, I ask for your assistance and wisdom in caring for our great oceans. Please guide me to what is right for me to do at this time to help preserve the precious marine environment. Please give me a task in which I can serve to better protect the oceans and help fulfill part of my divine mission. I also ask for your assistance in calling out to the Mermaids and Mermen so I may interact with them frequently for the good of all. Thank you Sedna for your help."

© Wendy Andrew

119

© Jane Starr Weils

120

Chapter 12
Kelpies Of Loch Lomond

After my delight at meeting Mermaids on our last weekend away, I was really excited about our next trip to Aberfoyle in the Loch Lomond National Park. Aberfoyle is associated with a famous Fairy folklore tale and a hill called 'Fairy Hill'. It was after our visit to Fairy Hill that morning that I started to sense we may be meeting a new Elemental. I am now aware when it is about to happen because I find myself tingly with anticipation or a sensation of butterflies in my stomach even whilst just sitting having a cup of tea! That is what happened while we were sitting in the Scottish Wool Centre car park deciding what to do that afternoon and pouring over the map. I had it in my mind to visit the grave of the Reverend Robert Kirk, for another book I was working on, however my instinct told me we had to drive up to Inversnaig, at the top end of the loch. I had never been there before but from the map it did not look far and the scenery would be stunning. As we steadily drove along the road, with Scotland's Runrig appropriately playing on the car stereo I turned to Richard and said, "*I think we are going to meet something.*" He was now used to my predictions and we started to speculate about which Elemental type it could be. The road became a single track while vast hills and mountains were looming about us, casting their shadows onto our path. When we arrived at Inversnaig, there was little to the village. A huge hotel and car park at the shore's edge, a few houses behind it and a ferry boat moored to the pier, but the scenery was indeed stunning. After a drink to revive us we headed out into the grey drizzle.

It was a typical Scottish 'driech' day. Cloud was misting over the summits of Ben Vorlich and Ben Vane directly opposite, over the loch. The water level was high - a result of the persistent wet weather that had been sweeping the country all winter. Rain was lightly spitting, on and off, sending Richard back for the umbrella shortly after setting out, but the cold wind had eased and it was bearable to be standing on the pebble shore-line of the loch. I knew Loch Lomond was a hot bed for folk tales from bygone years and as I stood watching a boat bobbing up and down against the far shore, there was a magical feel in the air. I had experienced it last year whilst visiting a friend at Rowardennan, which is situated at the lower end of Loch Lomond. It was a beautiful summer's day. The magical feeling had been the same. As you know Maeve, the Fairy Queen, has been one of my guides. Standing by the water I became aware of her energy beside me.

I could not see her, I rarely do, but she began to talk and I listened intently, "*I have brought you to the banks of Loch Lomond to introduce you to a group of Elementals you have not yet come across. They are written about a lot in Scottish folklore, often showing themselves to people when inebriated. This is because the Kelpie is a very mischievous and teasing Elemental. They mean no harm, but they know if they show themselves to those in a particular state of mind, the next day the same person will just think they were being a very imaginative drunk!*" I had to chuckle at that. Kelpies are famous in Scottish folklore tales for that type of behaviour. They are believed, in these tales, to be a type of water horse. She continued, "*The Kelpie is a type of Sprite that only resides in fresh water. They are similar to the Mermaids, being the guardians of large freshwater animals in the lakes and lochs. The Kelpie is the Scottish tribe. Throughout the world they are called different names. The reason I brought you to Loch Lomond is because the largest tribe of Kelpies reside within this loch. This is why Loch Lomond has a much more magical feel to it than other lochs, with the exception of Loch Ness, which I will expand on later. The Kelpie looks whatever way you wish to see it, hence its mischievous reputation. All Elementals show themselves in a particular chosen form. However the Loch Guardians are shape shifters - beings able to change shape at will.*"

At the time I was receiving this message from Maeve, I thought Kelpies were water horses who turned into beautiful woman when on land. I had previously read little about the Kelpie but in nearly all the books I have read since this message, the authors write describing them having beautiful bridles which have magical powers and if one finds the bridle and places it over ones eyes it gives the wearer the power to see the invisible beings of the other realms; by which they mean of course, the Nature Spirits that are being described in this book. Maeve further informed me by the loch, *"All Elementals have this power of changing shape, yet few types use it. Kelpies do it for fun. There are over a thousand Kelpies in this loch. If you call them they will come and show you their different forms. More often than not the Kelpie will show itself as a beautiful young, willowy woman with long straight hair down to her knees, clad in floaty, shimmering material. This is why folklore in Scotland depicts mysterious Ladies of the Lake, bewitching young men to make them their wives. It is an Elemental with enchanting energy; however they may show themselves, particularly to women, as handsome young men. Kelpies are good luck Elementals. Like Fairies and Sprites they can grant wishes. They do not need to be told your wish; they possess the gift of being able to see your heart's desire. Once you meet a Kelpie and you have gained its trust you can work with it for the good of the water environment and yourself. It is now time for you to speak to a Kelpie."*

Kelpie Appearance

I was a bit in awe of what Maeve had told us when I saw four etheric heads surfacing out of the water. My clairvoyant vision still had not opened fully therefore I could only really see their outlines. But then I saw one rise from the water and sit on a big rock beside me. It has crossed my mind that many people might be scared of experiencing such a phenomenon, but I found the Kelpies' energy to be similar to that of the Mermaids. I have never felt scared being in the presence of any of the Elementals, all I have felt coming from them is love. It is now clear to me that any Elemental will engage willingly if you are sincere of heart and wish to help them to maintain the balance and harmony within the natural environment. The Kelpie I could see was beautiful.

She was tall but slight, had long straight hair and very long, slim legs. She sat perched on the rock very delicately with one leg crossed over the other. She began to speak, *"I have come to speak to you about my race. There are a few of us around you. I am sitting to your left and my friend Alfia is on your right. There are also two of us in the water."* I looked but I could not see them any more clearly than before. The Kelpie that was talking did not give me her name. I have never felt inclined to ask for one, assuming that if I should know I will be told. Bearing in mind Maeve's message to me I said, *"You have come to me as women."* *"Yes, we did not need to create an illusion,"* was the reply. *"You accept that we are here,"* she continued. I was mesmerised by the Kelpie. Her legs were so long, like that of a top catwalk model. *"That is why we can walk on land. We are not like Mermaids who are confined to the sea."* she added reading my thoughts. Kelpies are traditionally in folklore meant to be able to grant wishes, Maeve had alluded to that too, and so I asked *"Can you help me make a wish?"* The Kelpie who was talking asked, *"What wish? We know that your heart has a few desires. We can help you with your three wishes but first we must tell you what we do for the natural environment."*

I put my curiosity about the origin of folk tales aside and let her continue. *"We are the guardians of the loch. Our role is to protect the animals, fish and plants living within these shores. As overseers of these water Elementals, our role is to dispense healing and energies among the other Elementals and their charges within this loch. We are second to none in the Emerald Isles. Lake Windermere in the Lake District hosts vast numbers too. In England they are not called Kelpies. Our sisters there are of slight difference and do not have such powerful magical powers. This is to do with the energy differences between the countries. Scotland has a much higher energetic frequency within its land. The higher the energy frequency; the more powerful the Elementals are. Scotland has managed to keep areas pristine. It has a lower population density which is of great benefit to maintaining this."* This is true. Scotland has retained a lot of 'wildscape' and its population is only around five million people. Vast areas are virtually uninhabited. Human activity in much of Scotland has been curtailed by its topography; therefore many of the earth energy centres and ley lines remain untouched. I was realising that each Elemental group was handing me a piece of a big environmental jigsaw that was being completed by writing this book. They were showing me that they worked in tandem, their roles entwined. The world and Mother Earth was not complete unless all the pieces of the jigsaw were in existence within the correct order and place. It was all falling into place in my mind.

"We live in the water; we do not need to breathe. We swim with great flight and fluidity through the currents. Our main environmental issue just now is noise and vibrational pollution. Jet skis and motor boats put vibrations and frequencies that are not desired into the water environment. We harmonise their energies and vibrations particularly to help the other species that live underneath. Another way we help, is overseeing the construction of hydroelectric dams," she went on to say. Scotland produces 11% of its electricity this way. The first commercial hydroelectric dams were built in the 1890s. Dams were also built for water reservoirs from the 1940s onwards. These dams have huge environmental impacts affecting not only the flow of the river and the land that is flooded, but bird habitats are often lost as well as salmon spawning grounds. However the Kelpie introduced an additional issue, one that not considered. "Lochs are created where there were none before. New water bodies are created and part of our job is to heal and help the other Elementals who have lost their homes: Fairies, Imps, Wood Nymphs, Gnomes and Tree Spirits. Where land has been flooded, new Nature Spirits are required to work within that environment. You should always be able to tell a man-made loch from a natural one, from the energy emitting from its shore-line. This is because the land is not now as it was meant to be. Therefore there is an element of trauma present within that water environment." When something is created naturally, all the physical systems within are occurring naturally. For example, the bottom of a natural loch will be full of pebbles, gravel or sand due to the process of formation. On the other hand when a river is flooded, it silts over the fields as it dumps its suspended load, tending to consist of finer particles. The natural lochs in Scotland were formed after 'de-glaciation'. The man-made ones are generally a forced flooded river over farmland or rough grazing. This is not naturally how a loch develops, therefore the processes and cycles occurring within that water environment will not be the same, especially 'energetically' during the early stages. The Kelpie added, *"If you are near a man-made loch please channel healing energies to the Elementals within. They will be eternally grateful for the power being given."* Kelpies were famous in Scotland because of the folklore tales, yet seemed to have so much wisdom that they were not credited for and such a vital environmental role to play within Scotland. It was nearly 4.30pm and getting cold. The Kelpie had delivered her message, adding I could return and talk to them whenever I wanted. I watched as the two that were on the rocks jumped back into the water and all four disappeared. Heading back to the car I pondered on what we had been told. It was only days later the significance of what the Kelpie had said hit home.

Appreciation & Invocation

Thank you to Maeve who helped with this chapter. If you wish to communicate with Kelpies and other guardians of freshwater lakes, Maeve gave me this prayer to help you:

"Guardians of the Lakes I call out to you to let me help you with your job of protecting the freshwater environment. I have a love of water and all the creatures within and I ask you for a task that will aid you in your recovery and conservation of your beautiful environment. I wish to meet you and engage with you in healing this great planet for the good of all. I accept it is part of my Divine task to do this work or I would not be here looking to assist. I would now like my task to begin. Thank you."

Chapter 13
Titinius' Message

The day after I had met the Kelpies we decided to take the scenic route back to the Borders. I became aware of a change of energy in the car. I saw a massive Fairy appear in front of me who spoke in a full, motherly tone of voice. I asked this beautiful being who he or she was. She said, *"My name is Titinius. I am in charge of the Fairy Queens. I very rarely communicate with humans, usually Maeve and the other Fairy Queens do, so I have no need."* Adding that little was written about her in folklore and even less in spiritual texts. She continued, *"Although I am a Goddess in my own right, I am also in charge of all Fairy folk. My role is to keep order and harmony. I oversee all, and I work with Gaia and Geb on a daily basis to help right what is wrong with the world,"* she said.

The more I communed with Elementals the more references were made to Gaia and Geb; Geb being the male aspect of the energy of planet Earth. We have discussed Lovelock's Gaia theory before, and I have explained that I assumed the theory as fact as a student, although there were many arguments made against his belief of Earth as a self-regulatory system created to allow life in all forms to exist. I had at that time however only thought it meant physical life. Now Titinius was alluding to my growing belief that Gaia actually was concerned with the energetic balance and the Elementals. And it was the Elementals that allowed physical life to exist on the planet within physical conditions. As the air Sylph had said, they are guided by a source higher than themselves to create weather conditions and patterns like using tornadoes to regulate the atmospheric energy. I was now aware of a hierarchy within the Elemental realm which was as intricate and complex as our own physical one. Titinius' visit was short leaving me to ponder her existence and what she might impart in the future.

Re-appearance

Titinius returned later that week wishing to talk about the state of the planet and the energy centres beneath Scotland's two great lochs: Loch Lomond and Loch Ness. I had heard of energy centres (the Kelpies had mentioned them) but I did not know what exactly they were. She explained, *"Energy centres are special sites on land or under water where the energy of the earth deep within emanates from the surface. One should know when one stands on an energy site, unless one's internal energy systems are totally shut down, due to such things as drugs or medication. The Earth energy rushes into every human cell and heals people, helping them to function better. Just as it helps strengthen an animal or human it strengthens Elementals' magical powers also. Elementals will gather around their nearest ley line or energy centre, travelling sometimes vast distances, to get this healing strength."*

Archaeological evidence suggests that our ancestors knew about Earth energy centres and structures, such as Stonehenge, built on them to strengthen and anchor this energy. Titinius' message turned to how, humans as a race are now affecting these energy centres. She said, *"Pollution not only interrupts the physiology of the environmental systems but it also stops Elementals being able to heal or protect. Take a mining area like West Lothian, for example. When you drive through this part of Scotland or when visiting your friend in Whitburn, you sense that the energy of the place and its people is very low."* This is true; my friend lives in this part of Scotland. The area is very flat and was once full of mines and mining towns. It lacks the magical feeling of Perthshire, where I originate from. Perthshire is an agricultural area and with the exception of a few quarries no mining has taken place. I was eager to hear the energetic difference between these two places. *"Well, West Lothian has had its ley lines and energy centres blocked and disrupted by coalmining. The ley lines cannot flow along their invisible seams. Rubbish* (slag) *heaps are situated throughout the land, reminding everyone of the trauma that occurred in this area,"* she said compassionately.

I had never thought of mining causing landscape trauma in an energetic sense but of course it evidently does, as Titinius was explaining, by blocking the free flow of the Earth's energy. I asked her what we humans could do to fix this destruction we had caused. She said, *"Encourage lightworkers to do healing on areas. Send Divine love and energy to a particular spot to raise the vibrations of the area and call in Angelic assistance to remove the Elementals' trauma. All that mining does is to lower the vibration in an area energetically. All pollution for example is a low vibration. By this I mean that everything vibrates at a certain level. Humans who are healthy and happy vibrate at a much higher level than those who are sick and miserable. This is why, by changing your thought patterns to something positive rather than negative, it makes you feel better. Positive thoughts increase your body's vibration. The higher you vibrate, the happier you as a soul are inside a human body."* I pondered on this last statement. I had been seriously ill for four years. The medical profession thought I would die. They had no cure to offer, yet I kept a positive mind set and held a firm faith that I would make a full recovery. I wasn't sure how this would happen but something deep inside told me this illness was something I had to go through at this point in my life. I was not interested in spirituality at this time and although I was a member of the Church of Scotland I did not pray for assistance or think anything spiritual would help me. I was determined not to think negatively or to think 'why me?' I took comfort in thinking that if I was going through this that must be one less other person in the world having to suffer. Crying only made me feel worse. There was nothing anyone could do or say, so crying did not change anything.

As an athlete in my teenage years, I was trained in visualisation techniques and the use of positive affirmations. When I used these techniques prior to a big race I would run faster. I did not know at the time that I was manifesting my desired outcome. I just knew that it worked. So I started using the visualisations and affirmations again when I was in my bed. They helped me greatly. Titinius was now explaining that they were raising my vibration which then helped to fight infection. When I was fit and running fast I would feel happy and exhilarated. My body felt in sync with everything and it was like the cells were singing with joy at the wonderfulness of exercise and fitness. I also ate healthily and did not drink much alcohol.

My energy seemed boundless. But when I caught a cold, felt ill and couldn't exercise, everything in the world seemed against me and negativity crept in. There is a theory that all disease is caused by energetic imbalances within a person's energy system and manifests as a physical condition. So if your life is not in balance then your mental, physical, emotional and spiritual bodies will be out of synch resulting in problems manifesting in that particular area. I firmly believe that vaccination and medications reduce the vibration of the human body. If a person receives a vaccination that is too strong for their immune system because they are fighting another infection or virus, or just that their immune system had not developed from childhood properly, then major illnesses can result. In my case I had a weak immune system from a second bout of glandular fever. I then had the flu vaccination compromising my immune system so much that I could not fight the infection injected into me or any other infection I came into contact with. The vibration of my body dropped and because of this, as well as my physical illness and pain, relationships in my personal life also became strained. Spiritual literature teaches us that people choose partners and friends of the same energetic vibration. Not many people realise this and will often brand someone as 'boring', yet often they are just vibrating at a higher level than the soul in the other person's body. I was also aware that living in an area of low vibration, say near an industrial estate or landfill site, can make people ill by dragging down the level their soul vibrates at. Titinius' message was making me grasp the impact of human activity on the subtle energetic balance of the planet. The meaning of 'Global Footprint', coined by many environmentalists to get people to look at their consumption and the impact they as an individual and their lifestyle are having on planet earth, had taken on a whole new meaning to me.

Titinius' message continued, "*Any activity that excavates the Earth disrupts the natural energy balance in that area. Hydroelectric dams are another example. They not only disrupt the individual biological and geological cycles and systems but water has a different energy to land. If you flood land it takes hundreds of years for the energy systems to restore balance. Since the industrial revolution, man has tinkered with the natural systems too much. It is now of great importance that these systems get back into equilibrium. The energy flow around the planet must be recreated, particularly in the areas of mining and other types of devastation.*" My next question presented what was a serious ethical conundrum for me as I use crystals for healing, contacting Angels, Goddesses and Elementals and for spiritual protection. Most crystals are mined. I shuddered at thought of the destruction caused to energy lines in those countries. Titinius explained, "Yes, *mining for crystals causes severe damage in certain areas. Many crystal mines were energy centres. Originally the Divine encouraged people to find certain crystals and to work with them. However, crystals take millions of years to form in some places and if humans continue to plunder Earth's bounty it will no longer be able to provide. Do not be greedy. Just purchase and use what you need. Send healing thoughts and divine light to the areas the crystal was mined from. Be very grateful for the gifts that crystals offer you. You live in a world where it is impossible not to consume, however it is now time to heal the planet of the wounds generations have inflicted on it.*" And with that she disappeared, leaving me to contemplate.

Appreciation & Invocation

To invoke Titinuis for assistance she suggested that you raise your vibration to as high a level as possible by thinking loving, positive thoughts on a daily basis. Although she may not be as forthcoming as other Goddesses she wanted you to know she hears all and will respond to any calls for assistance, often working behind the scenes to assist. At this time she is greatly concerned by the need to raise the energetic vibration of the planet and will assist all who wish to help her with this task.

© Myrea Pettit

132

Chapter 14
Energy Line Guardians

Titinius' message about the state of the ley lines in mining areas reminded me that I had not spoken to any Gnomes, the ley line guardians. The first Gnome I saw was in the wood near the house. The best way to describe him is as a small, dumpy little man wearing a hat running as fast as his legs could carry him to escape a chasing dog. The dog being Romany of course! As Romany had said, he just chased the Gnomes for fun, and he lost interest quite quickly whenever a scent trail took him off somewhere else. I had a good idea now where to find Gnomes in the wood as there is an area that Romany is always desperate to get to, often standing, watching things unseen to human eyes. The Gnome I spoke to was cheerier than I had expected. Their energy is very different to Fairies and Pixies, for example. It has a density; they feel more solid, perhaps because they are not so boisterous and playful.

The Gnome agreed to give me information and walked with me to a comfortable place for me to sit. Height wise, he came up to my knee. He had quite a gnarly nose, a beard and wore a hat just like the ones you will be familiar with on garden Gnomes. He started by explaining the different roles Gnomes can have on Earth, "*Gnomes, along with Elves protect the under-growth. Certain birds, such as pheasants, have Gnome guardians too. Our main job however is to protect the ley lines and Earth energy centres. We have the task of ensuring energy along ley lines are kept clear. We also have the ability to pump up the energy of the lines to make them more powerful at certain times of the year. The energy comes up from Middle Earth and Gnomes harness energy into their spiritual bodies and distribute it to the Pixies, Elves and other woodland Elementals.*" How fascinating, the more Elementals I spoke to the more evidence of the interconnected roles for healing and protecting Earth was coming to light. The Gnome exuberantly said, *"Ley lines are our source of energy. For example Fairies get energy from the moon. Waters Sprites receive it from the rapids. Sylphons get energy from the Tree Spirits. The trees also get energy from ley lines direct from their roots under the guidance of their Tree Spirits. The Tree Spirit then harnesses the energy to the Wood Nymphs and other Elementals, as well as in the atmosphere for the air spirits."*

It appeared from his explanation that all Elementals receive this Earth energy through an intricate system within their realm. I could tell that he wanted me to understand what an important job he and his fellow Gnomes had in the guardianship of the Earth energy. He continued, *"We are guardians of sacred sites also. For example Stonehenge in England, and the Ring of Brodgar in Orkney, Scotland, are built on Earth energy centres. The ancient Celts who built this ring (the Ring of Brodgar) communed with the Nature Spirits. Gnomes would have told these dwellers of that time that by placing the stones in the concentric circle in the way that they did, it would create an energy vortex over that ley line and energy centre. This would activate powerful energetic frequencies within the land to create a type of whirlpool effect that would spiral up into the air and increase the frequencies of that island and land within, thereby safeguarding them against destructive energy which they would perceive at the time to be flooding, drought or pest invasions on their land."*

At this point I had not read much about Earth energy from the spiritual angle. I had studied it at university and stone circles in my environmental archaeology course, so I was finding what the Gnome told me very interesting. The ancient civilisations were dependent on the land for survival so they were often very superstitious, using rituals to protect their land or request certain weather conditions and using other techniques we today would consider pointless in the modern era with our advancement in understanding through science. The Gnome further explained to me, *"Later stone circles were built across many landscapes up near the Scottish Borders, but not on such a grand scale, to prevent diseases and harness energy for the land they lived on. The ancient civilisations knew* the benefits of harnessing powerful energy under the soil and to bring energy into their crops and dwellings and also to protect against what they perceived as evil," he explained.

Gnome Stones

There is an area in the Borders, near Peebles, called the Meldons. It is a hillside with rough grazing and a very energised stream, or 'burn' as they are known in Scotland, running through it. The power of the ley line that also runs along here is so great; one can often get a hit from it when in the car driving past. There are stone formations which have evidently been purposely placed. I wondered whether these were an example of what my Gnome friend was talking about. As I was pondering this, the Gnome shifted round to the other side of where I was sitting and was examining the stone I was sat on. He then said, *"Throughout these woods you will find lots of Gnome stones."* I had never heard of Gnome stones before, except my friend Leila had recently had a dream about Gnome stones which we had discussed. That was three nights prior to me meeting this Gnome.

So I asked him what Gnome stones were. He told me, *"Gnome stones are what we call energisers. The stream that runs past the cottage is lined with stones placed there by ancient dwellers to increase the purity and energy of the water for drinking and medicinal purposes. Gnome stones have concentric curves (hollows) carved out of the stone. Originally these occurred naturally after the process of 'glaciation'. Erratics which are big boulders, seemingly randomly dumped by a glacier on a hilltop or a slope are also actually power stones. You will know when you speak to the rock guardians. In what you call science, there is always an element of serendipity which cannot be explained by scientists. This serendipity is however an organised control orchestrated by Mother Earth otherwise known as Gaia. Everything happens for a reason in natural systems"* Serendipity just means that results or formats can occur for no scientific explanation, they just happen. However the Gnome was saying that this is not the case, it is just our modern science has not advanced enough yet to fully understand the processes on this planet. Erratics are a classic example as there is no pattern of evident explanation to why a glacier dumped them when it did.

What I found incredibly interesting, having studied physical geography, was that these Erratics were energy stones or anchors, but why the name 'Gnome stones'? The Gnome explained, *"The Gnome stones are powerhouses on which Gnomes dwell. We sleep in the curves in the rocks as a kind of bed. During sleep we receive transmissions in our dreams to tell us what the energy levels are and what one should be controlling the ley lines for the energy centre. We do not sleep for long, only a couple of hours a day."* I had never wondered if Elementals slept! The Gnome however was more intent on explaining their roles of working with the energy centres and ley line earth energy and said, *"Ley lines can become polluted. The biggest problem is when building takes place intensively over energy centres or ley lines. Forestry is another issue because trees can interfere in the energy flow along the lines when packed so densely. In the past the Celts in particular were very knowledgeable about energy lines and worked with us, often unknowingly, to create a better flow. In the Chinese tradition of Feng Shui, the energy is called 'Chi'. The Chi is important and it is not to become stagnant. When Chi stagnates bad energy occurs which creates a depressed system. Nowadays with streams so polluted and land filled with chemicals much of Scotland's energy lines are clogged. This matter can be rectified. Hopefully people will work to clear blockage in the energy lines near where they dwell. To do this it is a good idea to sort any pollution issues to the best of your abilities. Then ask the Angels to send in healing energy to that area, then send all the Elementals (especially the Gnomes) healing energy from within you. If you are skilled at clearing energetic blockages and boosting ley lines this will be a great benefit to the Elementals in that area. They will be eternally grateful for your assistance. If you genuinely wish to help they will come to you in whatever way you request."*

I wondered whether, as with many of the other groups I had contacted, there is a hierarchy within the group, so I asked him.

He said, *"The Gnome hierarchy exists because of the importance of the job we do. Our hierarchy is similar to the Salamanders; a ley line is divided into sections and the Head Gnome will guard that. He will direct the other Gnomes beneath him. He is the one who receives the communications to change the energy frequency in the line or centre and directs the rest of us. He tells the cleaning Gnomes when to clean and purify the energies. Gnomes also try to guard against human disruption of the lines. We try to dissuade humans from mining, building, and pollution with our power to influence humans and animal thought. However few humans nowadays properly listen to their inner wisdom or knowledge so this tool is less effective."* Prior to my illnesses I never really took time to listen to my inner voice. I was too busy working and studying. Now I am always listening. It is the only way to truly succeed in life. I now ask questions of myself I never did before. Will this make me truly happy? Am I doing this for me or because others want me to? Does this feel right? If you take time to be alone and ask those questions, clearing your mind of any thoughts, the answers will come. There was one last thing that I wanted the Gnome to explain; what did Gnomes stones do? He said simply, *"Gnome stones carry the frequency we put in and act as storage: like crystals do."* He finished by saying I should speak to an Undine; the Elementals that protect the ley lines underwater. I was aware of Undines because other Elementals had mentioned them. I had been led to believe they were very beautiful so I was looking forward to experiencing their energy.

Meeting Undines

The evening meeting with the Undines was not premeditated. We had walked to the stream flowing near the cottage. I could sense a presence in the stream. The energy was very soothing and more powerful than I had felt being near the Water Sprites. It was the Undines living in the stream. I asked Richard to go back to the cottage to get the notebook so we could write down their messages. *"We are glad you have come to talk to us at last,"* they said.

Quite a few Elementals have been saying that to me, as if I have not been coming to them as soon as they would have liked or I had not been aware of their callings. *"We want to explain our role in anchoring the energies within these waters. We have a similar role to Gnomes as energy clearers. Our mission is to anchor the energy emanating from deep within the earth into the flow of the water. This is why some waterways are described as energised water. This magical energy can then be taken up by the other Elementals of the waterways. Our job also entails looking after and tending to plants that grow on the riverbed."* This had answered a question that had been in my head for a while. Do Fairies look after under water plants? The Undines had just satisfied my curiosity.

I wondered how the Undines worked with the Water Sprites. They answered, *"Our relationship with the Sprites is that we exist in harmony. We facilitate the water energy purification that the Sprites do by providing the Sprites with energy from the ley lines."* This coincided with what the Gnome had explained; Elementals working together in energy exchange. Although I could hear and feel the Undines my eyes could only pick up on flashes of movement. *"We are like Mermaids except we are thinner and have more sinuous bodies. That is the physical form we choose to take. We are larger than Sprites but smaller than Mermaids,"* one Undine explained to me. I was curious to find out how many Undines lived in this stream. She informed me, *"We do not reside in the vast numbers as Sprites do. This stream is highly energised because human populations created it so. As you can see Gnome stones line the path of the stream from source, at the top of the hill down to where it joins the River Tweed. Past civilisations worked with us to anchor the earth energies so this stream is energetically, very powerful. Can you feel the power as you descend into this glen?"* My answer was yes. The spot felt incredibly powerful; I had experienced the sensation of energy rushing into every cell in my body.

She spoke again, *"You will always feel more energised after visiting such a location as they were designed to anchor the Earth energy for* that population at that time. The plants, animals, and humans who dwelled there will all be fitter because of the purity of this water, air and the surrounding land. This then increased the vibration of the area. The higher the human body vibrates the less ill health will be suffered. Negative thought forms such as jealousy, greed, and anger along with fear all lower a human being's vibration. A soul wishes to vibrate at as high a level as possible in a human body. Early civilisations knew this and erected areas such as this to raise the vibration and ward off disease. Nowadays this is all long forgotten. It is important at this time of evolution that humans remember these methods of landscape management. It is time to activate the dormant ley lines along streams. The planet is suffering such great environmental damage, we need help once again to anchor and project this powerful Earth energy that is available to all in the Elemental world and to the human being, to restore harmony and balance in the Earth and thereby over turning the environmental damage. We wish you the best in your venture and should you have more questions please call on us again," she finished. With that I felt the energy recede. They had delivered their message and it was a very powerful one. I believe the early civilisations were more advanced than we are. Their understanding of the rhythms of the natural world is evident in the archaeological evidence and the Elementals were now drawing our attention to it. The messages they were imparting were now clear. The planet needs our help now. The Elementals need our help.

Appreciation & Invocation

Thank you to the Ascended Master, Serapis Bey for his help with this chapter. He works with protecting Earth energy and the Devic Kingdom and was worshipped in Ancient Egypt and later in Roman times. To work with Serapis Bey call him by saying:

"Dear Serapis Bey. I ask for your help in activating dormant Earth energy around my house (or at your favourite spot). Please guide and assist me in my task and give me any task you think I can do to help the Earth at this time. Thank you Serapis Bey."

Original Artist Unconfirmed

Chapter 15
Mineral Kingdom Elementals

I thoroughly enjoyed studying geology at university especially the practical sessions and the lectures on crystals. The beauty of the crystalline structures under a microscope and the vibrancy of the different shades of colours of the various mineral types hold an allure that is at times truly mesmerising. Of course at the time I was studying I was not aware I was tuning into the different frequencies each crystal holds and projects or even that I was benefiting from their healing properties, which I knew nothing of. During my first year I realised that science, especially with regard to the earth and environment was largely guess work and proposed theory. There is so much about this great planet we do not understand. I have found it totally fascinating that there is this whole energetic, environmental operation at work that is currently unrecognised except by a few enlightened souls. Yet all this made complete and utter sense to me. Yes, bits have made me stop to think and take a look at where my beliefs had come from but I am very glad of this. I do feel that I now have a greater understanding and respect for the natural world. I now look at a plant and recognise there is a Fairy living on it even if I cannot see it. The wonder and magic that the natural environment held when I was a child has returned. I now marvel at a tree I see everyday, actually appreciating its beauty whereas before it was just a tree. Now it is a home to many Elementals as well as physical creatures. The environment seems to be alive again, the enchantment of childhood has returned to me and I hope by reading this book, to you too.

Throughout the course of writing this book I have also begun to wear, carry and work with crystals. One of their uses is to help me communicate better with the Elemental Kingdom. Yet it was quite late on in writing this book before I had the thought of who looks after the mineral kingdom? Does anyone? To my surprise this Elemental was inside a donut shaped red/cream Jade crystal that was attached to my new red Chinese notebook! I could sense that there was an Elemental there. What kind I did not know, but its energy was very excitable. So I decided to just go for it and ask who was in this crystal. I heard an excitable squeaky voice speak back, *"I am a Crystal Being. I live in this crystal although it is quite rare to find a Crystal Being in a crystal this small."* Wow, I thought, a being that lives in crystals! He said, *"No other books on the shelf had a being in their crystal. We can talk to one another. I had a real job getting Richard's attention!"* I laughed; Richard had given me this book for my birthday, he'd said *"It took me ages to choose which one to give you. I kept picking up different ones but something made me go back to this one."*

Had this Crystal Being orchestrated ending up in my path? I was wondering at a lot of coincidences that had been happening to me of late. All part of the Divine plan I assumed! The Crystal Being started to have regular conversations with me when I picked up my book to write in it. One day he told me that Crystal Beings are just crystal guardians not rock guardians. Rock guardians are called Stone Beings I was informed. *"Stone Beings are older beings, although some Crystal Beings are old. We Crystal Beings aspire to become Gnomes,"* he explained. This was interesting because Gnomes are Earth energy guardians and the Crystal Beings come from a habitat within the Earth. From what I had been told by other Elementals they often aspire to be some other Elemental type as if there is an elevation process or a developmental transition to become certain types. The Elemental world was becoming even more fascinating for me. It seemed that as complex as the physical world is, with its feedback loops and interdependent systems, the energetic world is too.

I wondered how to care for a crystal for its Being's sake. I try to keep my plants happy and watered and fed for the Fairies that are on them and wondered if there was anything I could do for my new friend the Crystal Being. He said, *"We Crystal Beings are often traumatised when our crystals are mined. We have a network of friends within the crystal agglomerate. Please ask people to send love and healing to the crystal they are working with. You will notice the strength and power of the crystal increases when the crystal and its Crystal Being is happy.*" So I asked if he was happy. He said, "*I am very happy in this crystal although my crystal could do with being cleaned more often.*" This was true. Crystals need to be cleaned if you use them for healing purposes or even just as ornaments. I had not consciously done cleaning on this crystal because it was attached to my book. There are various ways of cleaning crystals. The methods I use regularly are the salt soak and the sunshine method. The salt soak method involves filling a basin or bowl with clean water and adding a teaspoon of salt. I use sea salt for this. You then place your crystals submerged in the water and leave them for a few hours. Not all crystals can go in water however, so check that the crystal you wish to clean is not one that dissolves. I also ask Archangel Michael (the powerful protector Angel) or the Fairies to come and remove all negativity, darkness and stress from the crystals. When you take the crystals out and dry them you will notice a difference.

I often see that they look cleaner and with renewed lustre and they certainly feel more vibrant. The other method involves setting your crystals outside in the sunshine or moonlight for at least four hours. Again I ask for Archangel Michael's help to re-energise them. Again after this care these crystals are more powerful and vibrant. It is important to check if the crystals you are putting in the sun are not ones that will fade in sunlight such as Amethyst and Citrine. If that is the case you can put them out at the full moon instead or don't leave them out too long in the direct sunlight.

Crystals For Elemental Communication

I have already mentioned I use crystals to help me communicate with the Elemental realm. We talked about Rose Quartz in the Unicorn chapter but there are other crystals that I use on a regular basis. Firstly I will explain how to use your crystals for this purpose then I will tell you about the various types you may choose to try with. It is important you get to know your crystal of choice. Spend time holding or wearing it. Then go somewhere outside where you will not be disturbed. Sit and quieten your mind. Close your eyes and take a few deep, slow breathes to relax you. Notice any thoughts or feelings that come to you. Listen to any voices you hear and pay attention to flashes of vision that appear through your third eye. This is you tuning into your psychic gifts. You may wish to dedicate the crystal you are holding to the communication with the Elementals. If so hold the crystal in your non dominant hand, and place it above your heart. Ask Archangel Michael to bless and protect your crystal. He is an expert in the removal of negative energies and emotions. Ask that your crystal be infused with Divine white light. Then ask the crystal to help you open up your communications with the Elemental realm. If it is a particular Elemental group you wish to use this crystal to work with name the Elemental group.

It is rare to find a Crystal Being in your crystal but if there is one you can ask it to help you with your communications. It is important to reiterate again that we all have different psychic skills but we all have them. You might find the crystals will help you see things with your third eye for example or your intuition might improve. Perhaps like me you will find you are clairaudient and can have chats with the Fairies and other Elementals because you can hear them. You might be able to feel the emotions of others or subtle energy changes, or just 'know' things without knowing why. Ideas and knowledge might just appear in your mind. These are some of the blessings that can then help you in every day life in various situations. It is likely that you will find out what your Divine mission is while working with crystals which will bring you much joy and happiness.

One of the best crystals to start working with I think is clear quartz. It is a very versatile crystal, easily available and relatively cheap to obtain. Crystals are formed within the earth when minerals are allowed to grow unrestricted. They naturally form a set of faces. The shape and colour of the crystals varies dependent on their chemical composition. Quartz is the commonest mineral on the earth's surface and takes a variety of forms. Clear Quartz is water clear in colour. It helps to accentuate any feelings, experiences or visions in the sixth sense as it is a stone of clarity. The element it is associated with is the storm element. It is also the easiest crystal to programme and work with. Therefore it is a good crystal to begin using to contact Elementals. It is nice to wear or hold and to generally have around your energy field and it is an amplifier. Another good crystal to wear or have in your house is Amethyst, also a form of quartz. Amethyst is violet or purple in colour and is formed when ferric oxide mixes with the silica. Amethyst is known as a powerful healing stone and is thought to ward off ill health. I wear an Amethyst ring (given to me by my parents) everyday for that reason. Its purple colour is also an indicator that it is a stone of spiritual protection. It is associated with the wind element. It is a good starter stone to work with particularly if you wish to communicate or work with Fairies. Flowers Fairies I have found are particularly attracted to its frequencies. It is also a good stone to use to develop your clairvoyance, so helping you to see the Elementals.

Currently my favourite crystal is one that I only recently started working with consciously for Elemental communications and is called Amazonite. I say consciously because I had been wearing some unnoticed in a bracelet along with Amethyst and Clear Quartz for some time. Amazonite is a green colour heading towards turquoise. It falls under the Alkali Feldspars category. It is known as a stone of truth, helping you to communicate your heart's truth and it is associated with the water element. Amazonite will help you tune into the Elemental realm very effectively particularly if you are clairvoyant. It will help you get a clearer view of the Elemental you wish to work with. The energy of this stone is also very soothing I find. I also find it helps with Mermaid and Undine communication. Rose Quartz is another common stone used for Elemental communication. It is a beautiful pink colour, known as the stone of love and it resonates well with the heart chakra. Chakras are the energy centres within our human bodies. Each chakra corresponds to a certain colour and spiritual and emotional aspect. The heart chakra is concerned with our feelings and attitudes to love. To be clairsentient you require an open heart chakra. Elementals are highly sentient beings so they will communicate with people through the heart chakra. Carrying and wearing this stone will help you to open your heart and clairsentience up to the Elemental realm along with the Angels and Goddesses. Through radiating love to the Elementals, which this stone will help you do, you will find communications easier. You will be able to feel Elementals around you and tune into their energy.

Different crystals resonate well with different Elemental groups I have found. For specific communications with ocean Elementals for example, I would recommend working with Amazonite or the crystal Malachite. This is a semi-precious stone and it is a beautiful bright green colour. It consists of green copper carbonate. Malachite is especially useful for facilitating communication with Mermaids and Ocean Sprites. Another crystal I like to use is called Chrysoprase, also a member of the quartz group. This beautiful green crystal helps connect you to nature and is a good crystal to carry or wear for general Elemental communications. As is Green Aventurine, a form of quartz which I find particularly helpful for working with Plant Fairies and Tree Spirits. For communications with Gnomes and Elves the best crystal I have found is called Green Moss Agate. This beautiful stone assists in connecting to the earth energy and is a very grounding stone. Another stone you could try for this is Rainforest Jasper. Jasper is a microcrystalline variety of quartz. This crystal connects us to Mother Earth herself and aids with earth healing therefore connecting you to the Elementals that aid with this too.

For connecting to the Fire Elementals I use Carnelian it is a vibrant red/orange colour. The energy of this stone is very stimulating I find and it is believed to strengthen courage. You can also use Natural Citrine for connecting to the Fire Element too. Stones that will help in general to open up your sixth sense and communicate with beings in other realms are Moonstone and Seraphinite. Although there are hundreds of crystals, I think the best way to describe how you will know what stone is right for you is that the stone will call out to you. You may not hear words but you will just know through your intuition that you require the vibrational frequencies that particular crystal is emitting around you. I will often pick different stones each day to have with me. Some I will not use for months others I only use for short periods of time, while others are always around me. I carry them in my pockets, in handbags, place them in my bath, have them sitting about my house, particularly with the Amethyst. I have it under my bed to promote a restful night's sleep.

I have often been asked about crystals that help people to communicate with and understand their pets. For telepathic communication with animals the best stone I have found Angelite. Angelite is a blue Anhydrite and is associated with the wind element. It got its name because it facilitates communication with one's Guardian Angels. It is sometimes known as the stone of Telepathy, which is when you can communicate through, thought alone as Romany does. Another stone you could wear is Apophyllite. Especially the clear variety as this has a very high vibration. The higher you can raise your individual vibration, the easier telepathic communication is. Having the stone Selenite placed in various locations in your home also helps with amplification of any communications your animal is trying to make with you psychically. Selenite is a beautiful clear/white stone which helps with spiritual activation. Other crystals are available if you wish to look more in depth into using crystals to commune with Elementals; however these ones I find are good for starting with.

Stone Beings

Although crystals are the headline grabbers of the mineral kingdom with their sparkle, lustre and beauty, rocks are what make up the surface of the earth. They also have great variety in mineral composition, appearance and degrees of hardness. They are in essence a collection of minerals which have cemented together. The Crystal Being had told me that rocks had different guardians to crystals. So I decided to find a big stone thinking it might have a guardian in it. I am now able to use my clairsentience to know where there is an Elemental Being about. I sensed there was one in a large stone I came across, so I asked it politely to speak to me. Unlike the Crystal Being, the voice that replied was not squeaky. *"Stone guardians are called Stone Beings. We enter into the rock regardless of their size so, for example, if a piece of rock breaks off the main stone then a new Stone Being energetically enters that stone. We do not enter rock dust. The stone needs to be in a solid form for us to enter. Generally Stone Beings will have more powerful energy the bigger the piece of stone or rock. Stone Beings are very different to Crystal Beings. As the rock guardians our job is to not only energetically protect the rock but also to give energy to rocks,"* he explained.

However I was confused. I had appreciated crystals as being 'alive' in a sense but to me a rock was just a rock and not a sentient being like an animal or a plant. The Stone Being explained to me, *"Gnome stones are energised rocks. It is the Stone Being that holds the energy and communicates with the Gnomes for the transference of this Earth energy,"* he continued. As if the Stone Being had been reading my mind, which he probably had, he added, *"Human beings at this time on earth, view rocks and stones as inanimate objects. This is not the case. They are sentient beings too.*

Trampling a flower has the same effect as crushing a rock or stone for their Elemental guardians. Some people who are in tune with Earth energies can feel the power within a certain stone. This in fact is the Stone Being that they are tuning into. Stone Beings are wise record keepers. We store data on almost all things. As Elementals we are known as the recorders of life on Earth. We are the records of the available Earth energies at any time since our geological formation. Ancient civilisations, such as the Picts and Druids in Scotland, worked with us a lot, often unknowingly, and we imparted much information to them about stone formation, ley lines and energy vortices. Stone Beings are energy carriers." I was fascinated by this revelation. I marvelled at the knowledge I could potentially get out of Stone Beings if they were a form of record keeper. Just think there must be lots of them at Stonehenge I thought excitedly and added that as a place to visit on my list. I was glad I had met the guardians of the mineral kingdom and I had a feeling I would work with them more in the future, for what I did not know. I could feel that this book was now nearing its end. Elementals were starting to give me messages that said this is not for this book, indicating more in the future. There was only one area left for me to visit I felt for this book and that would involve a trip into the mountains.

Appreciation & Invocation

Thank you to the Goddess Mawu who helped me with this chapter. Mawu is the African creator Goddess associated with the moon. Her role is to assist those keen on helping the planet, at the same time protecting its natural resources. She has an affinity for crystals and rocks which are the building blocks of earth. To invoke Mawu to come to your aid she gave this prayer:

"Powerful Mawu, great protector of this Earth, I wish to walk with you, hand in hand in protecting the planet. I ask for your assistance in working with the mineral realm for the gifts it can bestow on me and the healing work I can do for this great planet. Thank you Mawu for your love, assistance and continued support in all ways."

© Karen Frandsen

Chapter 16
Goharts And Mountain Guardians

Of all the landscapes in Scotland, the mountain environment is probably the harshest. The scenery of Glencoe and the Cairngorms is spectacular, some of the most beautiful in the world. It is largely pristine; too remote for most human interference. I knew this would be the last environment to uncover for this book, but it would involve a planned field trip up into the mountain region. I had no idea what to expect in terms of Nature Guardians. Then one evening, when Richard and Romany returned from their nightly walk through the forest, Richard told me he had seen a white light running away from him.

The energy felt so incredible and very powerful. This was interesting as only days before the gamekeeper had told me about the white light, he and other gamekeepers, had seen on this and other hills. The big ball of white light seemed to be running away as if they had disturbed it he said and they had all witnessed it clearly so knew it was not their imagination. Richard explained that the energy he felt was not threatening but was not familiar to him either. As Romany had been with him, and knowing he was a psychic dog who could see Elementals, I asked him what the light was. Romany replied, *"That was just the Gohart that lives in the hills,"* rather nonchalantly.

I had never heard of a Gohart so I asked him to explain what it was. He was playing and seemed none too pleased with my questioning but I persevered. He sat down and started to telepathically talk to me explaining that Goharts were guardians of the hillsides; the most famous was Pan! I had spoken to Pan already so I knew what Pan looked like. I asked if all Goharts were part goat and part human in appearance and Romany said, *"Yes, that is the form they choose to take."* I have now come to understand that each Elemental group choose their appearance so Fairies show themselves to us as having wings and dainty little bodies but really all Elementals are shape-shifters. It appeared only the Kelpies choose to change their shape at will, hence the folklore tales.

Romany explained that the Gohart is often present on their walks but chose to show itself to Richard tonight to draw attention to them as an Elemental group. "*Goharts are usually found running along hillside ley lines,*" he added. Romany had previously told me that telepathic communication was tiring for him because it required lots of concentration; I therefore left him alone to have fun with his toys and wondered when the Gohart would make his appearance to me.

A Visit From Pan

A few days later whilst lying in the garden getting some sun, Pan appeared by my side. I thought he had probably come to speak about the Goharts so I started to write down our conversation. He explained, "*Goharts guard the mountainside and oversee all who dwell in their environment. Can you now see each environment has an ultimate environmental guardian group? The Elemental world is tiered like the Angelic one.*" I had thought this was the case with what other Elementals had told me. Our Guardian Angels are watched over by the Archangels and there are Virtues, Dominions and Seraphim Angels in the tiers above them. Pan continued, "*I am the equivalent of Maeve. I do not physically reside on Earth in the Elemental realm. I am an intermediary between the world on Earth and the Deities in the sky.*"

Pan falls into the category of an Ascended Master, or Deity as he described himself. I have enjoyed meeting the different Goddesses and Deities whilst writing this book as much as meeting the Elementals. They have helped me a lot in my recovery, giving me personal advice as well as information on the Elemental Kingdom. As I looked back at the knowledge I had gained from them, the Elementals and the Angels, I was truly amazed by my spiritual journey.

Pan explained that these experiences were to continue and the more work I did on myself; letting go of fear, negativity and drama, the more highly I, as a soul on Earth, would elevate. "*You will have access to talk directly to Gaia herself,*" he said. "*She has agreed to allow you to communicate directly with her. You must however raise your vibration high enough to cope with her powerful energy. Like the Angels, who are messengers from God to commune with human beings, Gaia sends Maeve and myself to name a few, to communicate with the Elementals directly. Her energy is like what you call God and too powerful usually for direct contact. As humans increase their vibrations and reach new levels of consciousness, greater numbers will be able to communicate with the upper realms,*" he explained.

I understood this. Each time I did spiritual cleaning on myself in meditations, readings with the Angels, etheric cord cutting and chakra cleaning, my vibration raised and I could hear and speak to Archangels who I didn't have access to previously. Their energy would have been too powerful for me. Pan continued, "*Before you can speak to Gaia you need to be able to handle her energy. At the moment you could not. This is why you must work with crystals and Angels to elevate your consciousness even higher.*" Wow, I thought, Gaia must be an immensely powerful energy source, but then she controls and regulates all the systems on earth so she would need to be.

Goharts Explained

Pan then turned the conversation to Goharts, "*Variations of our species are based on regionality, but in essence we are all the same. We have the legs of a goat and the torso and head of a human. We have long horns that curve protruding from the tops of our heads. We have the hair of a goat. Our purpose is to combine the two races of the Animal Kingdom and Man. We protect the hillsides and the*

153

Elementals within. We liaise with Gnomes and help them anchor the energy from the ley lines. We do the same with the Undines in the stream. Romany and Richard saw a Gohart in the woods near the cottage the other night. We are such powerful beings that we often appear to humans as balls of yellow or white light, moving very fast across the mountain slope. Our energy is very powerful and can be felt from a long distance away. We are, however, shy Elementals who do not like to communicate with even the most esoteric human beings. We do not feel that is our role. We did however hundred of years ago share our knowledge and magic in Scotland with those you call the Celts and Picts. We taught them to work with the Gnomes in placing the layouts of geopathic stones. The purpose of this was for the rocks to anchor the vibrations being brought to Earth at that time, by Gaia's insistence that these vibrations be put onto the surface of her Earth."

The Celts and the Picts are the ancient dwellers of Scotland. They were perceived to be very in-tune with the land. Pan continued, *"Now is the time for this process to be re-enacted. New vibrations and frequencies are required at this time of great climatic and environmental change brought about by human folly. Rocks in essence are like sponges and coral is the same in the oceans. Coral in the ocean is where the energies and vibrations are channelled; remember your chat with the fish."* I had forgotten all about my visit to the North Queensferry Sealife Centre. We had gone there a few months ago. This particular fish had attracted my attention and I stood looking at it for ages. Then its Pixie guardian told me that it was a Coral fish.

The fish's Pixie told me, *"My fish's job is to keep the water clean. It is a purifier fish. It is important to purify the water because otherwise the fish would get sick. Our species' problem in the wild is that we are dying off because of the temperature change. My fish cannot tolerate major variances in temperature. The yellow fish with which it is sharing the tank can adapt over time. Yet my fish is dependent on the coral for its survival as a species, corals are purifiers too. What my fish's species does is take the frequencies from the coral and clear out the old frequencies no longer required. Few, if any, scientists know that this is my species role. My role as a Pixie is special because I tell my fish when specific frequencies are to be put out. The Undines tell me and then I start the clearing,"* the Pixie had explained.

Pan continued his message, *"Certain fish are used for that role in the seas to change vibrational frequencies. There are other Mountain Guardians you still need to meet. The Goharts oversee hill slopes but they again are part of a tier. You will find a powerful Mountain Guardian on Scheihallion."* This mountain is a Munro (above 3000ft) in Perthshire, Scotland and one of great geological significance. The meaning of 'Scheihallion' (a Gaelic word) translates into 'Fairy Hill of the Caledonians'. It was a mountain visible from the house I grew up in, its peak protruding up in the far distance. I was really excited that I was to write about Scheihallion. I had studied it at University.

In 1744 the Royal Astronomer Neil Maskelyne conducted mainly scientific observations on the mountain and was then able to determine the mass of the Earth. Following his survey, Scheihallion became the first mountain to be mapped using contour lines. Scheihallion's location is also special because the line of latitude is midway between the northern and southern points on the Scottish mainline and the line of longitude is midway between the most westerly and easterly points intersect very close to Scheihallion's summit, hence it is often described as the centre of Scotland. Pan left me that day knowing there must be something else special about this mountain that I had to find out.

Nine months later I received some more information on Scheihallion. This time it was from an Archangel called Morvosa. He told me, *"Scheihallion is one of the great powerhouses of the world. It is a powerful energy centre. The mountain has a unique shape and radial underground energy lines emanate forth from the mountain core. The structure of the mountain core is such that it powers a grid of energy centres throughout the northern world. Scotland has an abundance of energy. This is why the energy* of Scotland feels quite powerful yet unique. Scheihallion, Loch Leven and Mount Lothian are three of the pre-programmed energy centres which have the job of raising the frequencies within the planet.

The reason I wish you to go to Scheihallion rather than the other ones is because it is placed in its location for a particular purpose. Look at the map of Scotland, Scheihallion is as central as it can be. The reason why people have a fascination for this mountain is because its energy guardian is particularly powerful. The guardians of important mountains such as Scheihallion are not found in every mountain range.

Mount Everest is also energetically special as is Mount Fuji in Japan. Mount Rushmore in the USA, Table Mountain in South Africa, Mount Kilimanjaro in Africa, Ularu in Australia and Mount Ruapehu in New Zealand too.

These mountains all act as powerful energy radiators. You need to learn about the mountain guardians that protect the energy in the mountain core. Each core holds vast amounts of Earth energy that travels up from the mountain roots. It is not just the views that make people feel fantastic when they climb a mountain; they are receiving Earth energy from within the mountain core too."

I thought this Earth energy must be incredibly powerful having been taught that mountains have roots that are the same depth as the mountain is high. Archangel Morvosa continued to speak explaining that Goharts not only lived in hill slopes but on mountain slopes too, but the Mountain Guardian was different to a Gohart.

He added, "Scheihallion is very special because of the caves which allow people nearer the core, therefore they can get a bigger hit of energy. Ancient civilisations were well aware of mountain energy." I got excited at the thought of the caves as I had wanted to visit some caves to see what guardians lived there. Archangel Morvosa however, said I would not yet be able to walk so far as to get to them.

Visiting Scheihallion

Only a few weeks later I stood amidst the heather and boulders at the foot of one of Scotland's most famous mountains. As I soaked in the scenery; the distant hills and the forestry covering most of the side of Scheihallion's sister hill, I felt very grateful. It had been a long time coming: the feeling of the clear, cold, crisp mountain air on my cheeks again. It was nearly five years since I had been able to stand on a mountainside and feel the mountain energy deep within the ground filter up into my body.

I find being in the Scottish mountains very exhilarating; the feeling of freedom at the mercy of the elements and the deeper connection allowed with the Earth and nature. Although I grew up in sight of Scheihallion it was an hour and half drive away and I had never stood on it before.

The wind picked up as we ascended the path that followed beside the stream. We decided to walk off the path, which was very busy, being a Sunday, and we wanted to be undisturbed so I could connect with the Mountain Guardian I had been told about. What I saw when I tuned into the mountain was a vision of the middle of the mountain illuminated by a glowing white/yellow light that was radiating from a massive ball and going out up the top of the mountain. This energy powered all the ley lines for hundreds of miles around and then I got the vision of the energy travelling along underground seams crossing over all of Scotland.

The Mountain Guardian was showing me, rather than telling me, to protect our mountain environments because they are unique. I sat on a boulder and had a tingling sensation run through my body. I knew this was the earth energy powering up within. The activation of the mountain energy had started as if the Mountain Guardian had started to stir again. I had been told by Archangel Morvosa that I was a key for this activation process to occur. I had been advised that I would write a book on Earth energy in the future and I definitely felt a connection with this mountain. The Mountain Guardian did not appear like other Elementals however. Perhaps he was not one, but his energy was incredibly powerful, and the vision he had given me clairvoyantly was too.

I then heard a booming voice. Looking around to see where it came from I realised what I was hearing was not through my physical senses. I acknowledged the Mountain Guardian. He told me that Mountain Guardians only live in mountains of 3000ft or higher. They need to be over 3000ft to get the adequate 'height/root' ratio to be so powerful inside. He also told me that these mountains were reservoirs for Earth energy particularly when they were situated on an energy spot. The Mountain Guardian also showed me that the reactivation of the ley lines was essential at this time on Earth. This followed on from Titinius' message. I had always associated energy spots with volcanoes. When I was 21, I had spent 3 weeks in Iceland studying Hekla volcano for my dissertation. There the power and energy of the Earth is all around, you can't fail to feel it.

Now I could fully acknowledge, understand and respect the interconnectedness of planet Earth. All the systems were linked; hence the Elemental world was linked and worked together as part of a great team. The power of the Earth energy was more evident in the remote areas which have been left largely untouched by human activity. However humans are encroaching on these areas (recently there had been an outcry at proposed electricity pylons being placed around Scheihallion). The Nature Guardians had shown me the effect on humans when we are disconnected from Nature. I hope that this book will help people to reconnect with the aspects of the Natural World that they feel most akin to or even better, feel a part of.

Appreciation & Invocation

Thank you to Pan who helped with this chapter. Pan is available to help us all at anytime and all we need to do is command his presence and then he will appear. Also to Archangel Morvosa who can be invoked anytime for spiritual assistance.

© Linda Ravenscroft

160

Chapter 17
Guardian And Incarnated Elementals

Throughout the course of meeting the Elementals many of them told me I have a guardian that is their Elemental type. How can we have Elemental guardians when their job is to guard nature not humans? From my understanding some Elementals agree to be a human's guardian particularly if the soul they are guarding has a life mission relating to their element or they have even spent lifetimes on Earth incarnate in these realms.

Guardian Fairies

My first Elemental guardians that introduced themselves to me were my Guardian Fairies. I have two Fairies that look after and guide me. I discovered my Fairies when one time I was indoors and could hear a Fairy voice speaking to me. I looked around to see what plant they were on but it was then explained to me that this Fairy did not live on a plant because it was my Fairy guardian! Totally delighted by this revelation I started to invite them to guide me in my life and to work with me to help me get better, heal my heart and also help with my book. I was told early on that one of my Fairies was responsible for helping me with love relationships, her name is Romina. It was interesting because I have always been very discriminating when it came to relationships. Prior to the illness I had two 2-3 year relationships that were very loving. My illness put an end to the relationship I was in at that time but once I started to get on my spiritual path and told the Universe, the Angels and Fairies what I was looking for in a relationship, Richard entered my life. My Fairy who looks after my love life explained to me that Richard has a guardian Fairy looking after his love life too and our Fairies had worked to bring us together. One day I decided to ask Romina why she was with me and what Guardian Fairies do. She explained, *"I am the guardian of your heart. Obviously* you have Guardian Angels too who are concerned with your love life but as you are a special soul with lots to do in this lifetime it was important that you did not make any mistakes in that area of your life. A broken heart can always be mended but it is better for the heart not to get broken! Part of my job is to keep you away from negativity and be pure. I, along with the other Fairies you have in your bedroom, pluck negativity out of your heart chakra as you sleep."

I purposely sleep with flowers and a plant in my room at night for this reason. I did not know however until this moment that my Guardian Fairy helped with this too. I asked if everybody has a Guardian Fairy who looks after their love life. Romina said, "No, not everyone. A lot more people on Earth do however at this time because more lightworkers are incarnating with their task to help heal Mother Earth and the environment. A lot of these people are incarnated Fairies. We will explain more about that later. Some people however do have Fairies and will find that once they acknowledge their Guardian Fairy's existence and let them into their lives that much heart healing can be done. We are excellent at uniting soul-mates for this lifetime. Often it is blocks that are deep inside peoples' hearts that stop them from moving on emotionally and therefore inhibit their happiness and love life. Fairies are excellent at removing the blocks that stop people moving forward."

If Fairies are so good at this, then why is there so much misery in the world? I wondered. Although I was not directly asking her, Romina responded to my thoughts and I could feel her smiling at my naivety. "Most people have lost their connection with God, the Angels, Ascended Masters and other spiritual beings. They no longer remember that they are souls just residing on Earth for a brief period of time before they return home to the world of spirit. Because of this they forget why they are here on Earth and what they are here to do." I asked, "Why do we have to go through the veil of amnesia then when we are born?" (The whole point of the veil, as I understood it, was so we would forget about our life in the spirit realms in between incarnations.) "The veil of amnesia is designed to make the experience more testing. Most souls incarnate because they wish to elevate and the quickest way to do so is by being incarnate on Earth. Of course on Earth you have a physical body and can enjoy therefore physical pleasures that are not possible in the spirit world. This gives the opportunity for experiences not possible otherwise. Experiences and how the soul handles and develops through them is how the soul develops understanding and knowledge. However while on Earth with its many temptations and pleasure, people can become sidetracked and tempted by the lower emotions such as fear, greed, jealousy, envy and lust." Romina explained.

Then she continued, "Some souls need to learn how to overcome these negative, lower level emotions and it may take many incarnations until they get it right. Some people know they are on the wrong track and even the right path to follow but take the easy way out in their own eyes. Of course it is never easy and leads to often misery in the long run with the soul within yearning to be on its Divine path. Much of the Earth is waking up. Acceleration is happening as lightworkers and enlightened souls begin to remember their mission. Powerful souls with many incarnations, gifts and insight are incarnate on Earth. That was why it was important that we got you well and you wrote this book explaining what Elementals are and what we do. Perhaps if people reading this start to wonder what Guardian Elementals are and do and why they have them, they will remember more about their Divine path, get on it and follow it. It is important you teach people about this. Help them along with us, to remember why they are here and what they are here to do. Help them to find true love because the more we love, the more negativity and fear disappears. It feels great to be in love doesn't it? Would it not be great if the whole planet gave off that feeling and vibration? What a wonderful environment it would be to live in."

Filled With Love

I thought about this. I let every pore in my being, every cell in my body and every thought in my consciousness be filled with that feeling of love. I felt a wave of warmth and relaxation descend through my body and into my feet. The feeling of love being everywhere in the world was wonderful, and for a split second in that moment of time I could feel and see what the world would be like. What a wonderful place it would be to live. How happy the Elementals, plants, trees and all of nature would be including human beings. That glimpse showed me how earth was meant to be. Romina spoke again, *"Now you have felt and seen the vision, you can see how far away the planet is from that ideal. There has to be a change of consciousness, an elevation of thought and a move away from the 'drama' and 'self' dominating human interaction on Earth. It should be a place of love, not fear. The elevation process is accelerating. High frequencies are returning to Earth to be accessed by lightworkers. The Elementals are a large part of this ascension process. We hold vast amounts of knowledge, skills and healing techniques; however we are hampered by pollution and negativity. Just as humans are affected by low vibrations caused by negativity and fear; the effects of human thoughts, the Elementals are too. We rely on human beings for the co-guardianship of the planet. The higher the vibrations of the thoughts and actions of the 'collective consciousness' is the healthier and happier the Elemental Kingdom. It is not just the physical actions of humans that impact on our lives through pollution, disregard and greed but also the mental thoughts of the populous. The more people acknowledge the existence of the Elemental realm and begin to work with us, the more our powers return. We are more able to heal the planet, return it to balance and raise the vibration for the good of all living things."*

I had grasped fully what my Guardian Fairy was explaining to me. I could clearly see what the Elemental wanted to achieve and the joy that the world could hold if we raised our thoughts and cellular consciousness. The task seemed ominous, but not impossible. I had faith in the human race and I could see and feel the power lightworkers could hold to change the planet. I began really, for the first time, to think about who would read my book. I wanted to awaken souls who were waiting for the information but I wanted to attract those already on their divine path, working with Angels, spiritual healing and other practices of spirituality. I desperately wanted people to feel as

164

passionate as me about creating a planet full of love, happiness and high vibration. How exactly I could achieve this I was unclear. Yes I could write and give talks but would that be enough? Was that all I was here to do I thought? As I held that thought my other Guardian Fairy appeared in front of me. I speak to Eldmina a lot more than Romina but I actually did not know why she was with me. It had never entered my head to ask her! Again like Romina she patiently smiled at me then proceeded to sit on my left knee and say, *"My role as your Guardian Fairy is to guide you in your Divine mission. As your Divine mission is to work with the Fairies and other Elementals I am here to guide you if you need assistance and help. I work hand in hand with your Guardian Angels. As I am a Fairy I have an understanding of the Fairy world that the Angels would not. People who have Guardian Fairies are often very concerned by the environment, its welfare and feel passionately like Fairies do about protecting it. You have spent many lifetimes working with the Fairy realms."* Had I? Could that explain my playful, friendly nature? When at times I could be mischievous but not in a bad way? People have said I look quite 'Fairy-ish' at times because I am petite, slender and have big blue eyes. The Salamander said I was part incarnate Fairy. I asked Eldmina if she could explain what that meant.

Incarnate Fairies

Eldmina's explanation came, *"All souls originate from different sources and choose to spend their time in whatever realms and ways they wish. Being an 'incarnate Elemental' means that you have chosen to spend lifetimes in the realm of the Elementals; learning about their ways and their lives. One can then choose to incarnate into the human realm. You then have the added advantage of being able to see, hear and communicate with the Fairy realm as a human on Earth. You also choose divine missions which help the Elementals with their work. This is why you are passionate about the environment. There are lots of incarnate Elementals on Earth just now, and more coming in as the planet is nearing crisis point and needs the help of these beings in* incarnate form. Incarnated Elementals often take personal insult to the way people trash the environment or harm nature. Part of your task as well as to raise awareness of the Elemental realm is to direct incarnate Elementals into the ways of healing the planet. A lot of the incarnate Elementals at this time are new to being in human form and get side tracked by the many pleasures Earth has to offer. It is vital you start to run courses that will attract incarnate Elementals to help them with their mission especially by finding out the Elemental they have come from. Not everyone who is passionate about protecting the environment is an incarnated Elemental but they will have incarnated with the task of protecting a particular element or locality. Scotland as a country needs this work to begin quickly." I wondered why that is but no more information came. I have found that you don't always get answers to questions there and then, because it is not the right time for you to know yet but they are provided when it is.

Guardian Elementals

It was now 4pm in the afternoon, still daylight, a sign we were heading out of winter and approaching spring; my favourite time of the year. As I looked out the window at the snowdrops in the garden I wondered what other Elementals I had around me as guardians. Eldmina said, *"You also have a Guardian Mermaid who you have met, a Guardian Imp and a Guardian Unicorn. You also have two Guardian Sprites who joined you for this lifetime."* This was no surprise as rivers were always my favourite topic in geography early on at school. I also worked for RSPB Scotland as their Freshwater Policy Officer lobbying for better management and protection of the rivers. I wondered what I would do in the future that my Guardian Sprites would help with. I was curious to know what other people had as guardians. I asked Eldmina what Guardian Elementals Richard had. She said, *"Richard has two Guardian Fairies, a Guardian Gnome, a Guardian Merman and a Guardian Salamander."* Evidently Richard has been collecting Guardian Elementals too! The Gnome did not surprise me because Richard is really interested in Earth energy. The Merman was no surprise either really as part of his Divine mission is to help fish in fish farms with chemical-free pest control, but a Guardian Salamander was interesting. So I decided to ask if I could speak to his Guardian Salamander.

His Salamander was friendly and told me his name was Freidie and that his job was to keep Richard protected from fire. He said, *"Not many people are assigned a Guardian Fire Spirit. I have been with Richard for many incarnations now. Guardian Elementals like Guardian Angels travel with the soul when the Earth body dies into the next lifetime. I do not need fire to survive because I have elevated myself to guardian status. I am a being no longer dependent on my element. However, when my ward comes in contact with the element fire, it is my job to take over the protection role. I am the one who whispers instructions in his ear and drops thoughts into his head on how to escape or protect himself and his companions. In general we do not elevate to guardians, however many firemen who call for assistance or protection when dealing with fire may receive a Guardian Salamander. Many of those will have incarnated with a Guardian Salamander hence their choice of career. We look after the people who are trapped in burning buildings also and often someone who has escaped from a fire may find that they have a Guardian Salamander who guided them to safety when many others died."* I wondered if there was any way you could invite an Elemental to be your Guardian. Freidie answered, *"Yes, you can specifically call on Elementals to become your Guardian. However think very carefully and wisely before you do. Many Elementals are mischievous due to their playful nature. It would be advisable to establish a relationship with a particular Elemental. Get to know it before you invite it to become your guardian as this Elemental will then stay with you through all your lifetimes. Be aware, many Elementals do not wish to become Guardians as they are then no longer with their element. You would not wish to force any Elemental into becoming a Guardian unless they wish to do it."*

I was curious, what if you just invited any Elemental? How would that work I asked? Eldmina answered, *"Once you invite an*

Elemental to be your guardian they have to go through an elevation process to live in your energy field because in their current role as an Elemental they have too dense bodies. It requires the Elemental to lose the physical attachment to their element. The fact that a human has asked an Elemental to be their Guardian means automatic elevation for that particular Elemental Being. However remember what Freidie said that it is something to think seriously about. Is it for the Divine good or for selfish reasons? Usually if your Divine mission requires an Elemental Guardian they will be with you when you incarnate. If your mission changes for whatever reason a Guardian Elemental will just appear to help you. You therefore would rarely need to ask an Elemental to become your Guardian." I was really excited and fascinated by what I had been told about Guardian Elementals. I was sure there was more to find out but I was really excited about establishing a relationship with my Guardian Elementals like I had with my Guardian Angels and finding out more about what they could help me with. I was feeling by now that Guardian Elementals should be acknowledged as much as Guardian Angels are in spirituality. I decided to make it part of my mission (although I think it already was) to teach people about them and encourage people to work with theirs.

Appreciation & Invocation

Thank you to all the Guardian Elementals who helped me with this chapter. I asked if there was an invocation prayer people could say to start to work with their Guardian Elementals. Eldmina gave me this for you.

"Guardian Elementals I wish to acknowledge your presence and to work with you now. Thank you for your help that you have done unknowingly for me and I wish for us to start to have a relationship now. Please give me a sign that you are with me and guide me on my divine mission to help planet Earth. Thank you for all the love and support you offer me. I look forward to working with you from this day forth."

© Linda Ravenscroft

© Josephine Wall

Chapter 18
Gaia's Message

It was a lovely Scottish Spring day; the sun was out but there was still a cold nip in the air. I took Romany for a walk to the nearby stream whose banks were covered in little beautiful yellow flowers. The hills were clear in the background with some still white from the previous week's snow showers and the land seemed to be singing to me. There was a 'vibrancy' all around and the landscape was starting to explode into colour. The sound of lambs, newly born, bleating their little hearts out as they called on their mother for more milk, filled the air.

The Elementals were more active, their energy heightened as it always was when the sun came out. I decided when we got back from our little walk to sit in the garden and let the dog play with his ball around my feet, as he tried to entice me into a game of go fetch. As I sat letting the sun soak onto my face because I had recently read about the importance of sunlight and its healing effects, I became aware of a powerful but very loving presence around me.

I had been feeling particularly elevated spiritually of late and had taken to carrying Sugalite; a crystal that opens up the crown chakra just above the top of your head which allows you to access spiritual knowledge. When I enquired who this presence was, to my delight I was told, "*I am Gaia, otherwise known as Mother Earth herself. I am the consciousness of Earth, the beating heart within, the guide for all living creatures. I am assigned the task of guardian of the whole planet. My role is one of guidance, controller and reminder. My essence is the consciousness of love. I am the regulator of the checks and balance with in all systems of Earth.*"

So Lovelock was right I thought! Although I already knew this to be true deep down, it was nice to get confirmation from Gaia, Mother Earth herself. She continued, "*My male aspect is known as Geb. He is my yang, the masculine side to my energy for we all need to have a balance between the masculine and the feminine. I was closest to the human inhabitants of Earth during Ancient Greek times. They were a very advanced civilisation; they worshipped me and acknowledged all I did for planet Earth."*

I knew this to be true because I had read the Greeks believed Gaia existed before all of life and that she created life. The Greek myth about Gaia and how she created the world serves as a reminder to us of the interconnections of the world and the need to live in harmony and balance with it.

Gaia continued her message saying, *"My role is one that I regulate all the energy systems on Earth. The Elementals and Nature Spirits are my foot soldiers on Earth. They play very important roles to facilitate life on planet Earth as humans know it. The Elementals are 'key' to the continuation of survival on planet Earth and they are currently in great strife trying to cope with the conditions human activities have created at this time.*

Previous ice ages and major periods of climatic change were already pre-programmed and planned by the intergalactic council. Modern science as you call it on earth is not as advanced as you think. Yes there appears to be cyclical changes in conditions on earth in relation to the Milankovitch cycles and sunspot activity but this is actually all pre-programmed by a greater being (source) than yourselves on Earth can comprehend.

It is my job as guardian of Mother Earth to work with the guardians of other planets in your solar system and beyond. Sometimes things have to happen on Earth to benefit the other planets. It is important to comprehend that Earth is just one planet, and that beings live in other planets such as Pluto, Mercury and Mars but not in the physical dimension that humans live on Earth. There are many dimensions that life can exist in."

This did not surprise me. I have always thought it is arrogant of us to think that we are the only inhabited planet and it made complete sense to me that beings live in other realms on other planets, so did not need the same conditions to live in as we as a race did. Gaia was keen to impress her message however, so my focus was turned back to what she was teaching me. *"It is important that you convey to the readers of your book the important interactions that go on Earth. Every thought, every action and every intention you as human beings hold have a cause and effect reaction on Earth. Every time you disregard the importance of the environment, exclaim that it is not possible for Angels or Elementals to exist then you remove some of the available energy which the negativity you project destroys. Angels and Elementals are beings of love so it is important to treat them with love and respect for they do wonderful work on the Earth under my guidance.*

Elementals have chosen to come and reside on Earth and to fulfill their Divine mission; that of energetic purification and facilitation to allow life on the physical plane to exist. The Elemental groups all work as part of a team; they have no comprehension of self, so selfishness is not an emotion they feel. Humans can learn so much about how to be, by spending time with the Elementals and Angelic realms.

I thought this was so true. Even the way the Elementals all worked together, hand in hand, to ensure all the necessary functions, structures and balances were in place to facilitate physical life on earth. I thought what dedication they show us to their Divine mission. No place for egos, selfishness and other failings all too many humans demonstrate.

Gaia continued her message, *"At this time of spiritual awakening on Earth more and more humans are remembering their Divinity, remembering why they came to Earth in this incarnation and remembering the reality of the Elementals and the vital work they do. It is important people know who guards what environment and what help each group of Elementals require. Life on Earth is a precarious balance which can be maintained if humans respect the environment and acknowledge the impact they are having on the planet. "There is not much more to say except that the Elemental kingdom is of vital importance to the Earth. We thank you for raising its awareness and awakening old ancient knowledge that is within all souls. No Elemental group can exist without the other."*

With that Gaia was gone. Her energy removal seemed to leave a vacuum. I felt privileged to have spoken to her and proud I had raised my vibration high enough to communicate with such a great being. It had been a profound and incredible experience to find out about the Elementals; hearing their stories, feeling their energy and receiving their healing. A whole new world had literally opened up to me. I was nearly completely recovered and I had an excitement for life again. I understood better now my past, my passions and what I had to do in the future and all with the help of the wonderful guardians of nature known as the Elementals.

After Word

I sat staring out the window from my writing desk, looking at the garden. Leaves still littered the shrubbery and late snowdrops were peeking up in clusters adding some vibrancy to the Spring garden. A robin sat in the bush beside the wall and a blue tit was hanging on the peanut feeder, when out of the corner of my eye I saw the head of a pheasant. This pheasant often appeared with his beautiful iridescent blue, green and purple head shining out from behind the bushes he thought kept him camouflaged. I had not put food out this morning for him so he would no doubt head across the road in search of his oats. Although I watched him regularly, today he seemed to trigger a sadness in me that does not usually occur as I watch the birds. I had come to the end of my first book, but that was not the reason for this sadness that had descended upon me. It was just that part of my journey had come to an end. It would still continue I knew but it would take on another form, juncture and direction. This was also a time for me to reflect on where I had come from and got to in my life.

At the start it was all excitement, a distraction at times from the recovery and rehabilitation I had to go through. For the last year and a half the world of the Elementals and writing about them had been my focus. Now that focus had to change to make sure the messages get out there. The journey I have been on and have taken you with me through this book has reached its culmination. I wish you safe and happy passage in your exploration of your spiritual path and of the Elemental realm. May you have as much fun and feel as much excitement and joy as I did when I first encountered a Fairy and the many other Elementals written about here. Enjoy your adventures.

Alphedia xx

176

Acknowledgements

I would like to thank everyone who supported me while writing this book, especially the Angels, Elementals, Goddesses and Ascended Masters who gave me so much guidance, encouragement and assistance. Thank you to everyone involved in my recovery from a horrific illness that left me unable to do anything for myself and those who aided me in my physical rehabilitation: my parents, family, Joyce, Charlotte and my friends.

Also I have to thank the Prince's Scottish Youth Business Trust and the Scottish Business Gateway who gave me funding to set up Elemental Beings Ltd as a business allowing me to dedicate the time and energy to writing. Thank you to my good friend Steven Marwick who helped me with my website and encouraged me with my business. Especially big thank you to Kate Osborne, my editor, for thinking my manuscript was worth publication and for the guidance and support throughout the process.

Thank you to all the amazing artists who allowed me to use their beautiful images. Particularly to the artists who created images especially for this book - Hayley Rust, Leila Cattanach and Michele-lee Phelan. To Josephine Wall for allowing her 'Elementals' image to be on the front cover along with Leila for the design and knot-work. Thanks to Karen Kay and Barbara Meiklejohn-Free for their kindly given endorsements.

Finally this book would not have been possible without the love, help and support of Richard and Romany who encouraged me and believed in me when others didn't. If it hadn't been for Romany guiding me by asking for lots of walks I would possibly not have ended up in some of the locations where I had incredible Elemental experiences.

Artwork, Imagery & Contributions generously supplied by:

- Wendy Andrew   www.paintingdreams.co.uk
- Marilyn Alice Boyle   www.moondriftgallery.net
- Leila Cattanach   leilacattanach@hotmail.com
- Karen Frandsen   www.karenfrandsen.com
- Karen Kay   www.karenkay.co.uk
- Richard Kenchington   www.ribblepress.co.uk
- Judy Mastrangelo   www.themysticalvisions.com
- Barbara Meiklejohn-Free   www.barbarameiklejohnfree.com
- Myrea Pettit   www.myrea.com
- Michele-lee Phelan   www.dreamsofgaia.com
- Linda Ravenscroft   www.lindaravenscroft.com
- Hayley Rust   www.hayley-rust.com
- Josephine Wall   www.josephinewall.co.uk
- Jane Starr Weils   www.janestarrweils.com